The Science of Spirit

The Science of Spirit

Parapsychology, Enlightenment and Evolution

Luis Portela

Jefferson, North Carolina

ISBN (print) 978-1-4766-8389-8
ISBN (ebook) 978-1-4766-4152-2

LIBRARY OF CONGRESS AND BRITISH LIBRARY
CATALOGUING DATA ARE AVAILABLE

Library of Congress Control Number 2020048443

Front cover image © 2021 Natalia Sedyakina/Shutterstock

———

Printed in the United States of America

Toplight is an imprint of McFarland & Company, Inc., Publishers

Box 611, Jefferson, North Carolina 28640
www.toplightbooks.com

Table of Contents

Table of Contents

• 1 •

From Science to Love
(by way of introduction)

THROUGHOUT THE 20TH CENTURY, HUMANITY MADE enormous progress in science and technology, enabling our current dominion over matter in general and a good knowledge of the human body in particular, generating a huge leap in average life expectancy at birth. In 1900, for the world's population, this was 30 years; in 2019 it was 72; for the Japanese, Australian, North American and European populations it was around 80. People live longer and with more material comfort.

However, the existence of one or more non-physical entities within human beings, life beyond physical death, and the so-called parapsychological phenomena all have gone relatively unstudied, allowing for little spiritual clarification. It might even be said that the passion for the discovery of matter put an even greater focus on materialism. Thus, there exists some imbalance in a considerable number of human beings who are highly focused on the physical world, on what they have, and on how they appear; who give less importance to universal values, to existence, to spiritual life.

Therefore, many other people currently support the need for humanity to return to the importance of what moves them, creating conditions for more focus on such universal values and on living in harmony with those values. The results of scientific research in parapsychology over the last few decades are sufficiently important, though, that science is obliged to continue research in this area, in order to contribute to the spiritual enlightenment of humanity. A true scientist must never say again, *a priori*, that parapsychological

1

phenomena do not exist. On the contrary, the scientist must study and investigate, demonstrating, through the rigor of scientific methods, what is true and what is false, and how things work and why.

That will be a contribution towards enlightening humanity from a spiritual point of view. It would be reasonable to admit that some traditional psychic phenomena we hear about are pure fantasy, and clarifying this would bring to an end certain myths and the exploitation of people's ignorance of such phenomena. But it is also reasonable to consider that some of these phenomena will be confirmed as true, permitting a more complete perspective on ourselves and, probably, creating conditions for humans to assume greater capacity for their individual and collective fulfillment, through the possibility of using less-recognized forms of energy. It might even be possible that such wider, more encompassing perspective would create conditions for us to understand ourselves as particles of "universal energy" that are interlinked. This understanding may develop into a greater respect for each other, a greater respect for universal values, and a greater respect for the whole.

It seems that in the 21st century, science may contribute to the spiritual enlightenment of humanity, creating conditions for human beings to live with greater spiritual comfort, so that humans may live in an environment of increased harmony, developing their capacity for respecting and loving themselves and each other in its most diverse forms; also developing their respect and love for the universal whole of which they are a part. This is what I desire and defend in this book. I seek to find where we stand in scientific evolution in some of the areas normally only included in parapsychological studies. It is not my intention to concentrate your attention on the latest research, but rather allow you to perceive where the broad guidelines may lead.

I also approach some ideas in the area of spirituality in what I intend to be an independent manner, avoiding influences from religions and doctrines which I respect but which I am not defending in this book. I wanted, in a simple way, to cross ideas and knowledge with the intention of facilitating the way to spiritual enlightenment, to a route which permits the acceptance of unconditional love or universal love.

I wanted to do so in harmony with the teachings of some spiritual masters whom I much admire, masters including Lao Tzu, the Buddha and Jesus. I wanted to write something that, in some way, was in keeping with these masters' thoughts. I think that these three great thinkers—among others—sought to alert human beings to the necessity of focusing their attention on their own essence, as a particle of the universal whole, in evolution on planet Earth. This is what I sought to do in the following pages. I wrote this book with the satisfaction of one who shares what he has learned. I sincerely hope that reading it is useful and pleasurable.

I thank my friends Dean Radin, Etzel Cardeña, Fernando Lopes da Silva, Mário Cláudio, Mário Simões and Rui Mota Cardoso for their precious support in reviewing my book and making suggestions for improvements, whether they agreed with what I wrote or not. Thanks to my collaborators Paula Guedes and Sylvie Marinho for the admirable support which, as always, they gave me.

And I thank my family: Ingrid, my wife and beloved companion in life. My parents for the way they—each in their own fashion—prepared me for life. My dear children, António, Luísa, Katia, Miguel and Marta, and my wonderful grandchildren, Diogo, Leonor, Matilde, Luísa, Marta, Caetana, Guilherme and Martim, for the loving care with which they surround me. Thank you very much for everything.

◆ 2 ◆

Towards Enlightenment

Serene analysis of the earthly journeys of beings such as Krishna, Moses, Zarathustra, Lao Tzu, the Buddha, Confucius, Socrates and Jesus allows us to understand the effort that each one of them made towards the spiritual enlightenment of humanity. They didn't say exactly the same things as each other, but their messages had a common basis, that of getting closer to total wisdom. They didn't act in the same way—rather, they acted in accordance with the habits of the eras in which they were living—but all knew how to assume exemplary behavior. Each of them left shining paths that allowed the following generations to take advantage of more evolved existential perspectives.

As an example, according to the Uppanishads, Krishna said, "Why should there be a reservoir when there is a flood everywhere?" Lao Tzu, in *The Tao Te Ching*, states: "The Path is complete in itself. All blessings come from it, and it holds nothing back from anyone." The Buddha said, "The Path holds all things within Itself. Like the vastness of the universe, it lacks nothing, and nothing needs to be added to it" (*The Third Chinese Patriarch of Zen*). Jesus is cited in the Gospel of Thomas as saying, "The Kingdom of God is within you and all around you, yet you do not see it."

Curiously, it is not known if they had the intention of forming religious or doctrinal groups. However, their followers—in some cases—organized and constituted very diverse religious groups and sects, currently numbering over eight thousand. The messages that were left were, and are, very beautiful, but not all followers knew how to live up to them. Often they were misrepresented by some followers, who surrounded them with a panoply of myths, superstitions, taboos, rites and forms of business that have nothing to do with the messages of enlightenment of the masters.

Thus, on one hand, it was possible for humanity to evolve from its adoration of nature (animism) to its adoration of diverse divine entities (polytheism) and from there to the adoration of just one entity (monotheism), albeit with different names: Jehovah, Allah, God, etc. On the other hand, more recently, the scientific explanation of natural phenomena, which were incomprehensible to our ancestors, contributed to an evolution from subservient fanaticism to rational tolerance, and towards spiritual independence from the phenomenon of idolatry.

Comparative analysis of the different instituted systems allows us to conclude that, in essence, there is a common message that can be summarized thus:

1. The principle that gives life is in each and every one of us and outside of us; it is immortal and appears to be unseen, unheard and unfelt, but it is understood by all those who, in fact, wish to.

2. Each particle of this principle is also immortal and is undergoing an evolutionary trajectory toward total perfection.

3. Each human, being a particle of this principle, is responsible for everything that he thinks, says and does, and therefore for everything that happens to him [Collins 1952].

Recently, some religious leaders have made great strides in bringing their organizations together. It seems that if every one of the institutions could set aside whatever is not of primary importance, there could be a greater tendency for all to come together, above all in their ideas. The Buddha said, "Blessed are those who know, and whose knowledge is free of illusions and superstitions."

The evolutionary effort that each being individually makes, and the effort that each one of those institutions should employ, could make it possible for all to meet at the common goal, which, ultimately, all seek or should seek—total wisdom. However, it is necessary for those who lie to tell the truth, for all who do trade to become idealists, for all who deceive or exploit to become pure. Only thus will humanity be free of lies, myths, taboos, beliefs and mystical practices. Only thus will humans give up asking or praying for the resolution of their problems, definitively becoming people who makes the effort to help themselves and others, by using the appropriate strength of thought, will and intuitive, creative and altruistic abilities.

Within this concept, each one of us comes to Earth the number of times necessary to follow our path to spiritual maturity. Then, each will undergo further evolution in other planes, planes still unknown to humans in this stage of development, on a constant trajectory towards total wisdom, to the absolute. The physical body will be for our true selves what our clothes are for our physical bodies. Each time we come to Earth, we use a physical body for some years, placing us in this material world.

Upon connecting to this physical body, we temporarily forget our former journey so that we may overcome diverse situations with greater ease, without being stuck to previous experiences. Thus, each of our earthly experiences is just a small chapter of a long evolutionary journey that we make from the nothing to the whole. Awareness of this journey is fundamental to understanding universal reality, for placing ourselves in this reality and for the enormous fulfillment found in using all of our available potential.

Some doctrines claim that each of us chooses the moment and place of our arrival on Earth. Within this perspective, it is we who choose our region, race, sex, social status, family and parents (Andrade 2001; Benner 2017; Besant 1995; Mattos 1983; Morales 2004). According to this idea, each of us, before coming to Earth, will have made an analysis of our own abilities, seeking to identify our less-evolved characteristics, with the goal of finding the most propitious environment for experiencing certain circumstances, which will permit us to acquire enriching knowledge in areas of greater personal weakness, giving continuity to our evolutionary trajectory towards self-perfection.

To acquire such knowledge, each of us must overcome difficult situations which, naturally, may involve some personal suffering. Suffering that will only last until individual attention and effort focused on resolving that difficulty will allow us the right to overcome it, followed by the fulfillment of a duty accomplished. The more difficulty, the greater the sense of spiritual richness acquired. The sensation that this internal enrichment is true and definitive (for everything and always) minimizes or eliminates whatever we previously considered to be difficult, complex, and sometimes almost insurmountable, and motivates us towards the acquisition of new knowledge, towards seeing the necessity of overcoming other difficulties as a positive thing and, at the same time, towards experiencing, once again, some suffering related to our other weaknesses.

This perspective is criticized by many and not accepted by the majority, including by those who think there can be no knowledge without brain function. But it places the responsibility on the individual. According to this perspective, there is no reason to rue the environment in which we find ourselves, since it was we who chose it. We had the free will to select the place where we were born, foreseeing the kind of possible experiences we would find in that life. And we maintain our free will, which allows us, in any moment, to direct ourselves to where we believe we should go, thus being the ones who are primarily responsible for what happens to us.

While we are children, the responsibility for what happens to us is shared with our parents. But having chosen those parents—taking into account their characteristics and how they might or might not help their children—nobody should complain about the lack of support from their parents. Apparently, spiritual enlightenment brings a complete assumption of one's responsibility. The more enlightened a being, the more he assumes responsibility for what he thinks, what he says, what he does and, finally, for what happens to him.

• 3 •

Particles of Energy

WE CAN SEE HUMAN BEINGS AS PARTICLES of energy—small particles of universal energy: "As above, so below" (Hermes Trismegistus). Small particles of the universal whole, mirroring in themselves the characteristics of that whole (Eckartshausen 2003).

In the words of the North American thinker Harvey Spencer Lewis (1930), "Man is essentially a soul clothed with a body, and not a body animated with a soul." It seems to be almost the same thing, but they are two very different concepts. If we see ourselves primarily as physical bodies, perhaps animated by a particle of energy external to us—which some may call the soul, others the spirit; some believe it is just one body and others believe it is several—we tend to focus on the physical body and on matter in general. Although we may admit that there is a non-physical reality, we end up living focused upon material things.

However, if we see ourselves as a particle of energy, which temporarily inhabits a physical body—in principle, for some decades—we tend to assume a broader, more holistic, more complete view. We tend to consider the relativity of the material reality, keeping universal dimension and universal values present. The focus of our attention is on universality, taking into constant consideration the material reality and the nonmaterial or spiritual reality.

It doesn't mean that the spiritualist tends to undervalue the physical body and the material life. The respect for universal values and the profound sense of responsibility that the spiritual perspective offers allow us to assume, naturally, a balanced management of our earthly lives. We understand the necessity of looking after our physical bodies, so that we can maintain them as appropriate vehicles for this planet. We understand the advantage of tolerantly respecting others, in their various forms, and nature in general, seeking to be in harmony with the universal laws. And we gradually come to understand the advantages of living our day-to-day experiences in a responsible way, seeking to do our best, framed in a process of truly enriching learning.

Scientific circles in general ignored this spiritual perspective for a long time. Classical physics didn't have an explanation for it, but, in my opinion, quantum physics opened a window for the exploration of this area, reinforced by the theory of superstrings by John Schwarz and Michael Green (Green and Schwarz 1984a, 1984b; Green, Schwarz and Witten 2012a, 2012b; Schwarz 1998, 2010). According to these scientists, the smallest material particles known to humans, such as the electron or the quark, are after all constituted of energy in the form of extremely tiny vibrating strings or filaments. When these filaments of energy have a low vibrating frequency, they constitute material bodies. When they have a high vibrating frequency, they constitute diaphanous bodies. Joining this knowledge with that of the area of spirituality, it might be proposed that the soul or spirit is one of the latter cases.

These ideas correspond, in some ways, to what Albert Einstein proposed in the first half of the 20th century: that everything is energy. We can, then, consider that everything in the universe is energy, from the most diverse celestial bodies to the totality of earthly existence. Water and air are energy. Minerals, plants and animals are energy. The universal whole is energy. Apparently separate entities, we are after all beings made of vibrating energy, interconnected with everything that exists in the universe.

Maybe light is the subtlest form of matter, and maybe matter is merely the most condensed form of light. Both are expressions of the same energy or force of the universe according to the formula proposed by Einstein, $E = mc^2$, where E is energy, m is mass and c is the speed of light. Regarding visible light (a tiny portion of the electromagnetic spectrum), it is so subtle that it can only be seen when it interacts with other physical systems. The vast majority of the electromagnetic spectrum is invisible, outside the range that the human eye can detect, such as infrared and ultraviolet light, or x-ray radiation.

Since antiquity certain kinds of radiation have been reported, invisible to most people, emitted by living creatures, especially by good beings, sometimes considered saints, with whom is associated the idea of a golden or silver aura. Kirlian photography—although viewed with skepticism by the scientific community—seems to permit the physical detection of some of these radiations (Duerden 2004; Kirlian and Kirlian 1963; Marino, Becker, Ullrich and Hurd 1979). Kirlian photography is an electro-photographic technique developed in 1939 by the Russian physicist couple Semyon and Valentina Kirlian, who photographed colored radiations, considered to be vital energy, around physical bodies, namely plants and animals, and including humans.

This technique has recently been developed for use in medical diagnostics. An updated version of electrophotographic method is called Gas Discharge Visualization (GDV) (Korotkov et al. 2010; Moura 2000). In 1995, the researchers Roland Decaix and Claude Labroille registered a patent for equipment that measures what they claim is a vibrating energy emitted by material objects. It is understood that this technique is still to be perfected, which seems likely to happen.

It has also been reported that when an individual meditates, or by any other means manages to reach a state of spiritual elevation, he seems to become luminous, as if an interior sun is illuminating him from the inside. When the human reaches great levels of goodness, or pureness of thought, he seems to make his own light, his whole physical body radiant, but also illuminating his path, to better discern and intuit solutions most appropriate for continuing his own trajectory, as well as supporting those who surround him in their own evolution (Besant and Leadbeater 1901). Achieving such a state appears to be possible for anyone, of any social class, with any level of education, with more or less good health. There is an evolution of a growing light, the change produced by force of will and developed by the warmth of feeling, based on elevated thoughts. It is an enlightening light, a light of peace, of harmony, of love. Some call this spiritual light, others call it astral light, among other names. Many say that it is no more than a belief of some credulous people, but others associate it with a great amount of knowledge, and they consider that we are all submerged in it. Those too distracted by the materialistic life have failed to appreciate it because they have obstructed their own capacity for understanding spiritual light. The spiritualists consider that each person, evolving towards self-perfection, wins the right to be more in symphony with universal energy, becoming progressively more a vehicle through which it serves the self, others, and the whole.

Or, citing a quote attributed to Pierre Teilhard de Chardin, Jesuit thinker, "We are not human beings having a spiritual experience. We are spiritual beings having a human experience" (Covey, 1999, p. 47).

· 4 ·

Consciousness

C ONSCIOUSNESS SEEMS TO BE THE TOTALITY of experience in
the transient psychic life, in its continuous flow (Tart 2009),
and which manifests itself in abilities to receive, organize, integrate
and respond to internal and external stimuli; it is the notion—more
or less clear—that we have of psychological phenomena which oper-
ate in us and the capacity to understand and judge our own attitudes.
It is a permanent reality, encompassing all past and present phenomena, through which a multiplicity of states are reduced to just one
self. It constitutes the maximum personal oneness and identity.

In the second half of the 20th century, some in-depth studies
were made on the biological mechanisms in which consciousness is
involved, namely the hippocampo-mammilla-thalamo-cortical cir-
cuit, indispensable for short-term memory and, dependent on this,
long-term memory, through the use of the parietal and temporal
cortices. With the help of functional magnetic resonance imaging
(fMRI) and positron emission tomography (PET) scanning, the brain
areas related to the sensory organs were mapped, as well as related to
states of the different zones of our bodies and to reasoning, impacted
or not by emotions.

It is accepted that consciousness is not localized in one specific
area of the brain, but its functions activate certain preferential areas
of the brain, also generating participation by other associated areas,
something which is being studied in depth in the neurosciences.
Consciousness seems to act as the organizing principle of subjective
experience, which gives meaning and direction to the set of behavioral phenomena, controlling the neuro-physical processes that

happen in the brain, in the nervous system in general and, finally, in the entire physical body. This seems to be stable, active, differentiated, independent and vital (Eckartshausen 2003). Some consider it the true self; others give it other diverse names, such as soul or spirit. Some believe it to be immortal; others believe that it is limited to physical life. Some understand it as able to animate just one physical body; others accept it as being able to successively animate different material forms (Besant and Leadbeater 1901; Braude 2003; Damásio 2010; Delgado 1995; Hart 1967; Morales 2004, Osho 2004; Radin 1997; Stevenson 1997; Zukav 2014).

Some dreams and fantasies, usually undervalued, seem to constitute true memories of an apparently unknown past, which has led various authors to consider the possibility of achieving higher levels of consciousness in situations previously considered to be deprived of consciousness. The recall of supposed past lives, either spontaneously or induced by scientific methods, came to reinforce that possibility, especially when some researchers—such as Ian Stevenson and Erlendur Haraldsson—found historical records of facts, narrated by children who could not know in detail what had happened in other times and in places completely unknown to them and their families.

Some authors accepted different dimensions of consciousness and others came to speak of double consciousness: one would cover only the memorable data at brain level; the second would remain beyond physical life, assuming a universal dimension, possibly limited to its own evolutionary level. The difference between the two would result in the un-remembering observed at the time of birth, the forgetting of past experience and acting in accord with physical limitations. Within this perspective, the cases of child prodigies are explained as beings in whom this un-remembering has not been completely done, maintaining abilities acquired in previous lives. The same happens in children who recall supposed past lives and in adults who relate déjà vu phenomena, or rather, claim that they know, with richness of detail and obvious knowledge, places, situations or languages with which they have never had contact in their current physical life. It is not, then, a double consciousness, but a single consciousness, limited, from the beginning of the earth life, to the capacities of the physical organism being used. This is just like medieval knights wearing their armor and helmets, giving them limited capacities, being able only to see in front of themselves and with restrictions in mobility.

Full consciousness is assumed without contact with the physical body, whether in death, whether in displacement during sleep. In this case, there does not exist much memory of facts because the brain doesn't receive impressions about itself. And this full consciousness—which is defended here, despite being contested or not accepted by many—is a recognition of the self as a part of the whole, to which one feels indissolubly connected, in a relativization of earthly events, in the face of the absolute aspiration towards the infinite: of harmony, wisdom and love.

Altered states of consciousness are rare, and last just a few minutes or hours, either spontaneous or induced, without them necessarily being a pathological symptom. They may be induced by sensory deprivation (such as during meditation or hypnosis), by overstimulus or by hallucinogenic substances. In some cases, they can be unlocked by the person's own will. They are personal and, thus, subjective. Information gained from a state of consciousness may be specific to that state and may question the prevailing paradigms of logic, such as time and space, and of the consciousness of the self.

Altered states of consciousness may be considered pathological when they occur without being desired, assuming a dominant existential form, and provoking inappropriate situations in daily life. But the majority of these states should not be considered symptoms of illness, and may actually contribute to a better understanding of reality. Among the intense experiences sometimes referred to in these states are the feeling of being at one with the universe, the experience of contact with physically dead beings and the impression of understanding everything in a nonverbal way. But there have also been reported experiences of extrasensory perception, out-of-body experiences, and experiences of dramatic sequences which seem to occur in a different temporal context and are compatible with supposed past lives.

When a therapeutic intervention is necessary, many authors advise not interfering with the content, giving freedom to the imagination of the patient, and orientating him toward a dispassionate observation of the sensations and perceptions, without identifying with them, rather being a mere impartial observer. This distancing seems to permit an enriching understanding of situations and of their harmony with the surrounding reality. The individual enrichment possible from altered states of consciousness is used in some therapeutic approaches, ranging from hypnosis and relaxation therapies to past-lives regression therapies, independently of whether the descriptions are considered fruit of the imagination, or dramatizations of unconscious material, or even reliving of facts which may have occurred in the past.

The physician, scientist and thinker Abel Salazar (1915) spoke thus about consciousness: "This mysterious spectator watches from his hidden throne at the incessant glimmering of the mental flow, the uninterrupted current of sensations, ideas and judgments: because I am not my sensations, ideas and judgments, it exists as a difference in space, where they pass before my eyes, like before the eyes of the spectator, immobile at the margins, the calm waters of a river unfurl and flow." And, like him, the majority of humanity admits the existence of that self, which is considered true and named consciousness, soul, spirit and other designations.

The soul is the spiritual principle, the immaterial part of the human being and, apparently, of other animals. It is a particle of the whole, which can animate a certain physical body and exist after its death. It is a small part of universal energy which can return to successively animate other physical bodies.

Fifteen thousand years before Christ, human beings drew the soul in the form of a bird on the walls of the caves of Lascaux. In the East and in the West, the soul was identified as the breath of life. The Indian word *atman*, *ruah* in Hebrew, and *psyche* in Greek mean breath. The breath, when conscious, can center us in the moment, uniting the physical body and mind. In ancient Greece, the soul became an abstract thing, immaterial and immortal. For Aristotle, the soul "makes us live, feel and think." In the 17th century, Descartes separated the *res cogitans* from the *res extensa*, or rather, the spirit that can recognize from the object being recognized in its bodily expression.

During the 20th century, scientific and technological development permitted deeper study of the material body, almost ignoring the spiritual dimension. Human life was often understood as the interaction between matter and information, as if the human being was directed by neuronal and hormonal systems, determined by a particular genetic program. Accepting, however, that the organism cannot organize itself, some thinkers continue to defend that the soul is the organizational principle of everything that has life. Daniel Hell, professor at the University of Zurich, claims, "The soul represents that which men can only experience by and in themselves, in a way, first hand." For Hell, "The soul is the symbol of the living experience (psychic vitality)[...], and the symbol for unconditioned and in-the-moment experience (psychic existence) [...] and it is the symbol for what moves us in interpersonal relationships (psychic encounters)."

Most of humanity accepts the survival of the soul after physical death; this has been reported since antiquity and continues to be defended by most religions. Many Eastern religions maintain the theory of successive lives. In the Christian Old and New testaments there are also various references to reincarnation, abolished from the doctrinal concepts since the Second Council of Constantinople in 553; although the idea of survival of the soul was kept. Curiously, science was uninterested in the subject for centuries, creating great skepticism within academia and even a certain opposition to some initiatives aimed at studying observed facts, studies which began to be undertaken at the end of the 19th century.

Perhaps survival of consciousness after bodily death is the concept which has been less accepted in science, although it has been abundantly accepted in religion. Opinions continue to be divided as to described evidence, such as non-retinal images, reports made by the dying, the descriptions provided of near-death experiences, the cases of child prodigies able to execute tasks normally only done by talented adults, the reports of children who recall supposed past lives, and instrumental transcommunication with the capture of audio and visual messages apparently from a nonphysical origin. However, some researchers who have deepened study into these phenomena accept them with great conviction. Charles T. Tart, for example, claims: "I no longer *believe* in survival after death—I *know* my consciousness will survive death because I have *experienced* my consciousness existing outside of my physical body."

Regarding survival, as happened historically in other areas, existing prejudices and taboos will disappear to be replaced by deeper study of all described phenomena. Only thus will it be possible to separate the wheat from the chaff, identifying what can be demonstrated as true and discarding fantasies that have occupied many minds and, probably, disturbed the normal evolutionary trajectory of humanity. It seems, then, that a considerable scientific effort is justifiable for the understanding of spiritual survival.

• 5 •

Spiritual Evolution

WITH CALM ANALYSIS OF THE PRESENCE of beings on Earth, we easily accept continuous evolution, both materially and spiritually. Apart from biological evolution (Darwin's theory), a fantastic evolution of technology has become evident. A certain interior or spiritual growth, whether in individual or collective terms, may also be perceived. It seems we come to Earth as we go to school: to learn, from everything and from everyone (King 2009). To learn from those who know more, seeking to follow their good examples, and from those who, at the time, know less, seeking to identify their errors and creating conditions to not replicate those errors.

Each one of us is like a multifaceted crystal, with some facets still rough and some already well polished. Those around us will always have some facets more polished than ours and other facets rougher. Or rather, they always have areas in which they have learned and know more than we have, and others in which they have yet to learn. If we want to stay attentive and available to learn, we may see that there are countless opportunities for learning in our day-to-day lives.

We may learn when things go well, seeking to understand the reasons for them going well to keep us on the right track for future endeavors. However, we can also learn from the things that don't go well, by seeking the cause of the failures, and finding appropriate solutions and what should be corrected in the present and future. When we don't get tangled up in problems or pessimistic arguments, we are capable of thinking calmly, using the necessary energy for us to think clearly, and we begin to see an appropriate way of moving forward, and make the necessary effort to overcome such situations. We, therefore, are on an evolutionary path.

It may be claimed that the fulfillment of material opportunities pushes the person further away from his spiritual goals, or that the fulfillment of opportunities for spiritual growth should never have anything to do with material life. However, on the contrary, true fulfillment of material opportunities can only be achieved if spiritually well done; and the fulfillment of opportunities for spiritual growth will, most of the time, if not always, have had something to do with the appropriate management of material resources, be they plenty or scarce at the time. With the fulfillment of opportunities or the achievement of objectives, it is important to maintain a realistic and enlightened posture, avoiding disproportionate rejoicing, alterations in one's habits or foolish vanities. It's not worth losing time or energy in foolishness, as there are always new opportunities for learning which must be detected and satisfied.

As far as we understand, the laws which rule the universe are the same for all, permanent and immutable, making it really important to be in tune with them. Not because it is obligatory, but because it is the best way for each and every one of us. Complying with those rules translates as an enormous pleasure which clearly overcomes any delights in the exploration of physical senses. Not complying with those rules seems to naturally create discomfort, dissatisfaction, suffering. The greater the distance one is from universal laws, the greater the suffering. The more an individual makes others suffer, by the bad use of his free will, the greater the suffering for himself.

Suffering seems to function as a warning signal for the individual to awaken to the necessity for reanalyzing the situation and correcting his path, to seek better for himself, for others and for the whole. Depending on the level of enlightenment, it seems that what before seemed difficult becomes progressively easier. However, upon moving forward, new, more complex challenges appear, and a more refined sensibility in detecting new opportunities, and greater concentration of energy to satisfy them, seem necessary. As we progress, we also become stronger and more capable in continuing our evolutionary trajectory, as long as we remain attentive and open to such evolution.

At any point on that trajectory, it appears that thought works as a chain link, with primordial importance, that connects or attracts, although much of the time it is underestimated. The individual who thinks that what he does is very good becomes incapable of doing better (while he thinks like this). He who recognizes that what he does is not good, but is convinced that he cannot do better, becomes incapable of doing better (while he thinks like this). On the other hand, he who thinks that it is always possible to improve, and that the capacity for improvement is within his grasp, creates conditions for identifying errors, for enlightenment and for tuning in to universal values, all of which permit progress. Enlightenment obtained with humility, coherence and persistence generates levels of satisfaction that are never lost, or rather, it seems that this enlightenment becomes definitive.

In other words, light attracts light, generating a capacity for progress which, if used to its full advantage, allows individuals to realize beautiful, useful things and concretize their own evolution with great satisfaction, feeling that the progress made is definitive. Far from the pleasure of having, it is the pleasure of knowing and, finally, the pleasure of being. Of being what one idealized, of being equal to oneself and forever (at least in that aspect).

What is valid in individual terms is also valid in collective terms. Throughout the history of humanity, human beings focused much on the study of matter, were enthused by their ever-growing dominion over it, and overvalued it. Simultaneously, by not deepening their knowledge of the spiritual realm, they devalued such values, allowing for the material to impose itself over the spiritual (Beauregard, Schwartz et al. 2014). However, a growing number of people are getting tired of some of the absurd things that are commonly accepted, and some scientists are making themselves open to study areas in depth which, until recently, were considered taboo (Cardeña 2013, 2014; McClenon 1982). It should be taken into consideration that the increase of knowledge in the neurosciences and parapsychology provides data which demonstrate that some current positions are inadequate and favor the formation of a new perspective, less matter-based, of the human being on the surface of the planet, with a subsequent rebalancing of values, in tune with nature (Beauregard and O'Leary 2007; Kelly et al. 2007; Schwartz 2012; Tart 2009). Seen through such a perspective, huge shifts will not seem necessary for evolution to continue.

Nevertheless, if people continue to insist on enjoying all possible material comfort at their disposal, while stubbornly refusing to complement—in nonmaterial realms—the evolution they are making, mother nature may wreak a rebalancing in catastrophic ways. The bad use of free will, at a collective level, may push humanity towards large-scale military conflict or an ecological disaster, with eventually catastrophic consequences, forcing human beings to rebalance their values. It is understood that something has to improve in the posture that humanity has assumed.

It is desirable that all those that have the capacity to contribute towards peaceful change know how to apply their best efforts towards such. Worthy and beneficial acts generate satisfaction by bringing us a feeling of progress made. The more constructive actions we carry out, the more progress will be made. The better we seek to correct the errors of the past, the better the progress.

Suffering should not be considered inevitable in seeking enlightenment. Suffering may continue to exist while we do not correct the situation, while we do not exert the sufficient effort towards perfecting ourselves, while we do not assume a truly useful position for ourselves and for others, by thought, word and deed. We could consider suffering to be essentially generated by the person's inappropriate thoughts or attitudes in the present, as well as in the past, be it recent or distant, and, on the other hand, by environmental situations inherent to the development of life on the planet. When the individual is careless in the direction of his thoughts, words or attitudes, he becomes pernicious for himself or for others; he seems to be subject to suffering for a longer or shorter duration, until he begins to definitively correct each of his errors. It is said that this suffering may be provoked immediately, or it may appear later on. The defenders of the theory of successive lives claim that suffering, in some cases, relates to some questions relative to supposed past lives (Drouot 1996; Jesus 1973; Kastenbaum 1988; Mattos 1983; Morales 2004; Ramacharaca 1998).

Environmental situations causing individual suffering may be related to unfavorable options taken by the individual in the family sphere, in the business world, or in his leisure. On choosing adverse environments, he is susceptible to painful consequences. But suffering that originates from the environment may not have anything to do with isolated attitudes, being instead part of the normal development of events relative to the life of the planet, according to the options of others and natural laws.

It is not exactly that evolution is made through suffering but, rather, through favorable actions for the self and for all. The correction of errors is necessary but may happen by lucid effort of the individual, without the overwhelming presence of suffering. The happiness of constructive achievement translates as greater efficiency in purification through achievement relative to the purification through suffering. In constructive achievement, the human being feels the profound pleasure of the vibration that is synchronous with nature. Because, finally, evolution happens through accomplishment.

The theory of reincarnation, proposed by Pythagoras, Plato, Confucius, Lao Tzu, the Buddha, Nietzsche and Schopenhauer, among others, has an evolutionary nature to it, postulating that every particle in the universal whole makes a long journey which, on the surface of the Earth, will have begun in the mineral kingdom, then in the plant kingdom and, later, in the animal kingdom. This way, any one of us has already been rock, plant, later fish, then reptile, inferior mammal, more evolved mammal and on and on, successively, until we came to the planet as human beings. We came many times also as human beings—just as he who goes to school to learn—seeking to sand the roughness of the different facets of our being and, thus, becoming ever more perfect.

It seems that only a deep inner analysis, searching for greater comprehension of who we are and what are our real objectives in our earthly experience, will allow us to understand our role in the universal whole, creating conditions for developing the sensitivity, tolerance, compassion and wisdom that enable a superior degree of achievement. Therefore, it is advisable to achieve a greater inner self-analysis, of opening up the consciousness, to gain a deeper understanding of who we are and who we want to be.

Regarding access to universal wisdom, it seems that what is acquired along the way is kept forever. There is no atrophy from more knowledge to less, whether in individual or collective terms. The evolutionary trajectory we follow always has a positive direction. When each of us stagnates temporarily, it might seem that we are regressing, but we will only do that in comparison with those who continue to evolve, never in absolute terms. When humanity allows itself to be enmeshed in masterfully elaborated lies, or when it assumes somewhat primitive behaviors, it even seems to pass through periods of regression. But the regression will only be apparent in relation to the normal flow of things.

The human being who strays from his path, who thinks, says or does things that prejudice the normal evolution of himself and/or of others, will sooner or later receive natural warnings which allow him to rethink the situations and correct his route. These warnings, commonly identified as suffering, are often seen as unpleasant, although they ultimately seem to be beneficial in absolute terms. Also in collective terms, sometimes significant corrections of trajectory seem to be necessary. When human beings together stray from their natural evolutionary route, transgressing universal laws, it is perhaps only suffering—brutal in some cases—provoked by catastrophic situations, that awakens them to reality, inducing the choice to reassume the positive direction of life.

Will we, then, individually or collectively, be condemned to this or that situation of suffering? It seems not. We can always use our free will correctly and seek the path to perfection, before we are punished by nature. Thus we describe our evolutionary trajectory for ourselves. And the sum of the trajectories of beings found on the Earth translates as spiritual evolution for the planet, in parallel with its physical evolution. A trajectory towards perfection, but also one of discovering what is already more evolved, of what is better, superior and at which we haven't yet arrived. A trajectory of progressively nearing total wisdom, the absolute.

To evolve spiritually seems to be, at the same time, the development of a force in a positive direction and one which allows the truth to flow within us. Because, after all, total wisdom always existed. It is we who haven't yet arrived there. And, for us to arrive, development of that healthy effort towards perfection is essential. But that effort, in itself, is perhaps limited since we become excessively focused on ourselves. It seems necessary to maintain strong harmony with nature, confidently allowing the truth to flow. But, in fact, the truth also only seems to find conditions to flow when we make an honest effort to search for it, uncovering that which until that moment we couldn't see, although it was always there!

The fact that billions of human beings continue to suffer in poverty, hunger, oppression, humiliation and brutality seems to make evident that the central objective of the human experience should be spiritual evolution instead of mere physical survival. And, for spiritual evolution to become real, a deeper understanding of our being will be necessary, understanding how from our thoughts we can introduce improvements in ourselves and how those improvements might have an impact on the world.

◆ 6 ◆

Grains of Sand

SOMETIMES WE FEEL SMALL COMPARED to the grandness of a mountain or the immensity of the sea. We are surprised by nature and wonder how it all works, looking at the innumerable beings that abound around us. We feel even smaller when we see ourselves as small dots or grains of sand on the surface of one of the very many astral bodies that exist in the universe, itself also just a grain of sand compared to the universal whole.

Small in size and small in knowledge, we, however, are making an interesting and progressive evolution, acquiring knowledge, maturing ideas and perspectives, conquering the right to know more and more, and becoming ever more comprehensive. But sometimes the difficulty in making progress is great, and for truth to triumph, we need enormous persistence and great sacrifices.

Giordano Bruno (1548–1600) was an Italian philosopher who revolutionized astronomy, stating, "The Universe is infinite, inhabited by God and with an infinite number of stars, some of them inhabited" (Bruno 1984). Thus, he gave another dimension to Copernican astronomy; Copernicus had, a few years before, proposed that the Sun was the center of the universe with the planets revolving around it, including Earth. At a time when it was believed that the world was fixed and at its edges was a celestial dome, where there were to be found the Sun, the Moon and the rest of the stars, governed by a complex system of cycles and epicycles, the theories of Bruno—who was a priest—were badly received, strongly criticized and rejected. They were accepted only by small groups of thinkers. The majority did not agree, however, and contested his ideas. He was imprisoned by the Inquisition, which kept him incarcerated for eight years in Rome, where he was condemned to death by fire for refusing to give up his theories. Giordano Bruno accepted the papal decision with pride and serenity, and was burned alive in 1600.

However, some thinkers continued to defend his perspectives, including Galileo Galilei (1564–1642), who appeared in front of the Holy Office of the Inquisition six times, where he was coerced to deny his ideas to save his life. But the truth always wins in the end, and the teachings of Copernicus, Bruno and Galileo came to conquer public recognition in the second half of the 18th century when the system that they proposed became recognized as a better description of the laws of the universe. Copernicus is considered the founder of modern astronomy and Galileo the founder of modern physics. But Giordano Bruno came to be respected as a visionary with great conviction and coherence who, at 52, gave his own life so that the truth might triumph.

Earth is one of the planets of our solar system, where there exist at least sixty natural satellites that orbit the known planets, and a large number of asteroids and comets. But our Sun is only one of the estimated 400,000,000,000 stars in our galaxy—the Milky Way. The galaxy has the shape of a disc with the diameter of 130,000 light-years, and for the Sun to complete a single rotation around the nucleus of the Milky Way takes 225 million years.

The galaxies make up groups, some of which consist of 2,500 galaxies. The Milky Way belongs to the Local Group, one of the smaller clusters of galaxies, with only about 40 galaxies. It is estimated that in the entire universe there exist about 2 trillion galaxies, each one having thousands of millions of stars. Admitting the existence of some dozens of planets and satellites in orbit around each of those stars, we can conclude that the number of planets in the universe is fantastically huge.

In the last few years, astronomy has demonstrated the existence of thousands of planets outside of our solar system (exoplanets). Some of those planets are about the same distance from their sun as the Earth is from our Sun, possibly giving home to some life forms similar to Earth life forms. Obviously, it is also possible that on other planets in other star systems there are other entirely different forms of life, all still unknown to human beings. In the next few years, there will be telescopes launched into space that are thousands of times more powerful than the current ones on Earth or in orbit, such as Hubble or Kepler. With them we will be able to discover even more mysteries of the stars and planets and, eventually, of life.

If, one day, scientific proof of life on other planets is established, then the perspective of the human being about itself and the universe will certainly change, with some ideas fading away, and some taboos coming to an end. It has been a long time since it was considered reasonable that humans or Earth were the center of the universal whole. Today, we view ourselves as a small particle in evolution on Earth, which is itself a small particle in a solar system, which is in turn a small particle in a galaxy, and so on. Each particle reflecting the amazing potentialities from the whole.

It is reasonable to admit the existence of other forms of life on other planets, which can act as world-schools, similar to the role played by Earth. There may be forms of life that are similar, different, or very different. If we take into consideration the theory of reincarnation or successive lives, we might wonder about the existence of other cosmic planes where spiritual beings, free of matter, remain temporarily in between physical lives. Maybe they are there to make a complete overview of their evolutionary trajectory, analyzing what was done and what needs to be done, as well as preparing conditions for such.

Of course, what is referred to in the last paragraph is not scientifically demonstrated. Only some currents of thought and/or religions have raised the possibilities of this kind, but, in a holistic perspective, they might make sense. It is reasonable for us to expect and desire that scientific research deepens in these areas and brings us ever greater material and, above all, spiritual enlightenment. This enlightenment may give a more balanced attitude to humans, considering material and spiritual realities.

• 7 •

Thought Transmission

THROUGHOUT TIME, THOUGHT HAS BEEN accepted as a manifestation of spiritual ability directly related to intelligence. Through thought we discover, explain, and solve the most diverse problems that appear in our way, forming and combining ideas, meditating and creating images, with a constructive attitude for the present and/or the future.

Some theorize that, upon emitting a particular thought, we radiate a vibrating wave—similar to light or sound waves—invisible, but capable of having effects remotely. Some more sensitive people are able to, consciously or unconsciously, catch those thoughts, in what is called telepathy. Telepathy is the transmission of thought from one individual to another without any means of material communication. It is the sensation received by a person and related to an occurrence at that moment and at some distance, or in circumstances where the information from the other person is impossible for the receiver to know.

Most people spontaneously have, at least a few times in their lives, telepathic experiences. However, it is evident that in some people this characteristic is more developed than in others. Some authors accept today that it is a common characteristic in all humans and many animals, and it can be trained and developed. Each of us can be a sender and a receiver of thoughts. Some are stronger senders, some better receivers.

Some European and North American universities, in recent decades, have begun to study telepathy, not just in human beings, but also in various animals such as dolphins, dogs, rabbits, mice and chickens. Some of the experiments they carried out became well known. In 1973, for example, a multidisciplinary team at the State University of Leningrad, led by professor of psychophysiology Genady Sergeyev, carried out a surprising telepathic experiment involving the identification of objects. One of his collaborators, Yuri Kamensky, who was in Moscow, mentally transmitted the names of various objects to Karl Nicolaev, who was in Novosibirsk in Siberia, about three thousand kilometers away. Nicolaev was able to capture the mental information about the objects that were unknown to him.

Since then, many other studies have been carried out, the majority of which done at the discretion of scientific research laboratories. Although these concepts are still controversial today, and it is necessary to confirm them in a convincing scientific way, sooner or later they will be further disseminated (Chauvin 1986; Murray et al. 2007; Peoc'h 1988, 2001; Pérez-Navarro and Guerra 2012; Sheldrake 2011; Ullman and Krippner 1989).

In 2014, the English researcher Rupert Sheldrake ran a study in which 63 participants—people who claimed no parapsychological abilities—received telephone calls from four possible people, chosen previously by those who would receive them, but could not know who would be calling at any particular time. Before answering the call, the participant would take a guess about who was calling. Five hundred seventy trials were undertaken, in which the chance of guessing correctly was 25 percent (1 in 4), but an average percentage of 40 percent correct guesses was obtained. Following similar procedures, experiments were conducted with emails and telephone messages, in which results above chance were also obtained, on the order of 43 percent.

These tests of telepathy by telephone were replicated at the universities of Amsterdam and Freiburg (Lobach and Bierman 2004; Schmidt, Erath, Ivanova and Walach 2009), with similar results. Comparable experiments were also performed with emails and SMS messages, also obtaining similar average percentages of correct guesses. The author supports that these results demonstrate the existence of telepathy, because while dialing or writing a message to someone it is necessary to think about that person and these thoughts appear to be picked up by that person.

In 1979, Howard Eisenberg and collaborators did experiments on telepathic transfer of information. They gathered 52 volunteers—also people who did not claim parapsychological abilities—and paired them up, randomly assigning the role of sender to one of each pair, and receiver to the other. The sender saw a short film about a certain theme, after which he was presented with five photographs (one of which was taken from the film), which he put in order of relevance to the film. Simultaneously, the receiver remained in a room separated and isolated from the sender, any communication between the two being impossible.

While the film was watched by the sender, the receiver was invited to remain relaxed and to think about the other. Finally, the receiver was presented with the same five photographs, with the request to put them in order according to their experiences during the period of stimulation of the sender. This protocol was repeated in seven sessions, with a different film and different photographs presented in each session. A control group was also used, in which a similar protocol was applied to the receiver but (without the receiver's knowledge) there was no sender. The receivers of the experimental group selected the photograph from the film in first place more frequently (in 35 percent of cases) compared to the control group (in 25 percent of cases).

In 2010, Storm, Tressoldi and Di Risio did a meta-analysis of 29 studies similar to the above-mentioned study, but in which the receiver was placed in a situation of sensory deprivation (blindfolded and with headphones emitting white noise) with the intention of amplifying their receptivity in capturing mental impressions sent by the sender (this is known as the Ganzfeld experiment, with ganzfeld meaning "whole field" in German). The results, again positive and statistically significant, confirmed the possibility of extrasensory communication between two people. In 2013, Rouder and colleagues noted some methodological limitations in this work and adopted a different method to analyze the results, concluding that, in their opinion, the data did not demonstrate evidence of a para-psychological phenomenon. Still in 2013, Storm and colleagues published a new article, in which they accepted some comments, argued against some others, reanalyzed the data and obtained findings that supported their original conclusions.

In another line of studies, since 1963, several independent research laboratories around the world reported electroencephalographic (EEG) signals correlating between pairs of individuals, functioning as senders and receivers, placed at distance and totally shielded from each other. EEGs were taken simultaneously from the sender and the receiver, who were placed in completely isolated compartments. The sender was asked to try to stay mentally connected to the receiver and the receiver was asked to think about the sender and be receptive to any thought or mental image that might come into his mind. Both were asked to remain relaxed.

Then, the senders were subjected to stimuli, like light flashes or audio tones, which provoked in them certain alterations in their EEG. At the same time, similar alterations were observed in the EEG of some of the receivers, without them having been exposed to any kind of stimulus. These results, statistically significant, were obtained in various studies (e.g., Charman 2006; Duane and Behrendt 1965; Grinberg-Zylberbaum et al. 1994; Manolea 2015; Radin 2004; Standish, Kozak et al. 2004), but not replicated in others (e.g., Ambach 2008; Hearne 1981). Some authors (e.g., Acunzo et al. 2013; Kalitzin and Suffczynski 2003) further suggested some methodological limitations that needed to be mitigated to obtain solid and consistent results.

In 2004, Leanna Standish and colleagues obtained results of this kind in various pairs of volunteers and, in one case, managed to obtain similar results, using the technique of functional magnetic resonance imaging—fMRI (Standish, Johnson, Richards, and Kozak 2003). Those results were later reproduced in a follow-up study (Richards et al. 2005). However, Moulton and Kosslyn (2008), also using fMRI, claimed that they failed to detect any significant differences in terms of brain activity, when the receivers visualized an image previously visualized by the sender and transmitted telepathically to the receiver, or an image not seen by the sender. They concluded that they had not found any experimental evidence for extrasensory perception.

Over time, several researchers have noted that, in the kind of experiments here reported, better results could be obtained when the senders and receivers were family members or friends (Broughton and Alexander 1997; Playfair 1999; Sheldrake 2014). Some highlighted the tendency for better results among univiteline twins (i.e., those from the same zygote). It was also understood that some people with greater sensitivity, commonly called psychics or mediums, tended to obtain better results (Braud 2002). Since the end of the 20th century, experiments on transmission of thought have been carried out involving animals. These experiments are valued more highly in terms of public opinion for the fact that the animal in the experiment would have no intention of falsifying the results, that is, to cheat.

Such an experiment was conducted with dogs by Rupert Sheldrake (1998). He was intrigued to find that a significant number of people claimed that their pets predicted their owners' arriving home, often by waiting at the door minutes before their arrival. He decided to do experiments with dogs, placing video cameras in several rooms of the houses where they lived, constantly registering the dogs' movements; and simultaneously placing a camera with the owners of the dogs, to carry with them in their daily tasks, to provide a way to register the moment that they decided to head home, all in completely different situations and completely unpredictable schedules. Sheldrake demonstrated that the number of times that the dogs went to the front of the house to meet their owners just a short time after the owner had started to head home was statistically significant (Sheldrake 2011; Sheldrake and Smart 1998, 2000a, b). For example, in one experiment it was seen that in more than 200 trials, the dog seemed to anticipate the return of its owner in more than 80 percent of occasions, going to wait for him at the window.

This ability of some dogs (and other pets) to identify from

a distance the moment in which their owners decided to head for home can be interpreted as a process of thought transmission, or telepathy. Perhaps most people can unconsciously feel the effects of thought transmission, ignoring the reason, the origin and the mechanism. Some thinkers accept that, because of this, we sometimes find ourselves feeling down without knowing why, having been the target of someone's dark thoughts. In other situations, we feel surprisingly galvanized to develop a constructive attitude without understanding why, having been the target of some positive thoughts.

Strength of thought can apparently establish an environment that contributes to health or illness, happiness or sadness, triumph or failure, well-being or its lack. And its power can make us feel like this at limitless distance. This power seems to have characteristics which attract similar currents of thought and repel those that oppose them. Thinking bad thoughts, the being not only emits but also captures dark thoughts, at the same intensity, repelling good thoughts. On the contrary, valuable, courageous, firm thoughts attract thoughts of the same kind and repel negative ones, producing a confident atmosphere capable of leading to success.

We can, then, theorize the existence of spiritual networks of different levels. And it is possible to admit that when we think negatively, we tune into to spiritual networks of negativity. Thus, when someone thinks consistently in a positive way, he tunes in to spiritual networks of the same tone, which may strengthen his capacity for achievement by transference of information which he intuited and/or transference of energy from the global system. Access to the respective network is related to the characteristics of our thoughts, it being easier and stronger the more we focus our energy in a permanent way, in a determined tone. Not only do we attract the network with a similar signal, we repel everything with a contrary signal.

According to this idea, an individual will be very self-limited if, in general, he is ill-intentioned, only episodically wishes good for himself or others, limits himself to praying or begging for such, or even sporadically acts for good. On the contrary, positive thought, voluntarily and constructively maintained over time, may be the key to a successful physical and spiritual life, by permitting unlimited connection to universal wisdom. Most thinkers and teachers invite positive thought, repelling bad thoughts, and using strong will to orient their thoughts in a useful way for each of us, for all our fellows, and for the whole.

There have been many experiments in telepathy and psychokinesis (or mind-matter interaction) performed with humans and animals, which over time were conducted with increasing levels of scientific rigor and, thus, are becoming scientifically accepted.

◆ 8 ◆

Psychokinesis

PSYCHOKINESIS IS THE INTERACTION of a person with animate or inanimate matter, through the mere act of thought. Phenomena of this kind are also known as psi-kappa and may occur spontaneously, in an unconscious way, or in a deliberate and conscious way. It is not explainable using classic laws of physics, but it is speculated that it may be compatible with quantum physics.

The existence of humans with abilities to perform unusual mental phenomena, including in the area of parapsychology, is widely known. Some individuals who appeared to be especially talented became famous. Let us recall three of them now: Eusapia Palladino, Ted Serios and Nina Kulagina.

Eusapia Palladino (1854–1918) was an Italian medium, known for moving objects placed on a table, while seated on a chair with her back to the table and with no obvious means of physical contact with the objects; for making the same table levitate; for ectoplasmic materialization (a visible emanation emitted by the physical body of some mediums) and various other objects appearing from nowhere; and for trance mediumship, in which she would change personality and, for some minutes, apparently embody spiritual beings. Palladino was studied by various researchers, including at Cambridge University, in 1895, a time in which some members of the Society for Psychical Research considered her to be a fraud.

However, later, other researchers, such as the Nobel Prize–winner Charles Richet, carried out several experimental sessions with Palladino, reaching the conclusion that her abilities in psychokinesis and materialization were genuine. In light of the number of favorable studies, the Society for Psychical Research carried out a new study in 1908, publishing a robust report validating Eusapia Palladino's mediumship abilities. There was a consensus that she sometimes acted fraudulently—as happened, unfortunately, with other mediums too—but the existing data proved the veracity of most of the phenomena (Alvarado 2011; Braude 2015; Watt 2016).

Ted Serios (1918–2006) was a North American hotel employee who became well known for being able to impress images onto photographic film merely through the influence of his thoughts. From 1964 to 1967, the psychiatrist Jule Eisenbud supervised hundreds of experiments, witnessed by more than a hundred independent observers, many of them scientists. In the course of these experiments, around a hundred anomalous polaroid photographs were produced. Serios—without any contact with the polaroid camera, nor with its film—made images appear on the film of things that did not exist in the visual field of the camera.

Some skeptics criticized these experiments, believing that some kind of fraud was involved, though they could never work out how it was done. Eisenbud countered, showing that Serios could produce the same kind of images when he was placed inside a Faraday cage (i.e., he was shielded electrically), and with the camera and its film always on the outside of the cage and held by an assistant (Braude 2007, 2015; Eisenbud 1989).

Nina Kulagina (1926–1990) was a Russian medium who, starting in childhood, claimed to be able to make objects move without touching them, something that was filmed several times. Several Western scientists had the opportunity to study her performances up close. Among them was Joseph Gaither Pratt, of the University of Virginia, who, after carefully analyzing her demonstrations, certified her psychokinetic abilities. However, while in the several films made of Kulagina's performances no fraud was ever detectable, many scientists still doubted her abilities.

Nina Kulagina never exploited her abilities for commercial ends, which gave her credibility. Studies were done at the universities of Leningrad, Moscow and Prague on her ability to cure infected wounds and some diseases, but above all on her demonstrated ability to move objects by force of will, so-called psychokinesis (Watt 2016).

Scientific research in this area has been developing in the last few decades. In 1935 Louisa Rhine and Joseph B. Rhine studied the capacity of a person to mentally influence how dice landed when thrown. To exclude any cheating in the throwing of the dice, they were thrown with the aid of a cup or by using an automated machine. Before the throw of the dice, the thrower would say which number they wanted to be facing upwards, seeking to influence the dice with their mind. In a total of 6,744 throws, the Rhine couple (1943) observed that the desired number appeared 300 times more than might be expected by chance, a number that was statistically significant.

In 1991, Dean Radin and Dianne Ferrari analyzed 73 relevant publications, presented by 52 different researchers, from 1935 until 1987, involving 2,569 participants who tried to influence the result of 2,746,105 throws of the dice. The overall results were considered clearly significant and replicable.

Later, studies using random number generators (RNG) were carried out. In 1997, Robert G. Jahn and colleagues published a 12-year-long RNG study, in which 91 people had tried to influence the behavior of a random event generator with their thoughts. The machine randomly generated binary numbers (0 and 1), bits, in an unpredictable sequence, and with a tendency to generate the same proportion of 0s and 1s. The REG generated 200 bits per second, which according to chance should result in an average result of 100 (the sum of the 1s). In each trial, the subjects were asked to influence the machine to produce a greater number of 1s than expected, or to generate more 0s, or to not express any intention in order to establish a control baseline.

The results deviated slightly from the expected average (100), to 100.026 when an increase of 1s was intended and to 99.984 when an increase of 0s was intended. But given the enormous amount of data collected, this small difference was statistically significant, demonstrating that people were—by using thought alone—capable of influencing the machine. The difference occurred whether they were close to the machine or placed some kilometers away.

The Science of Spirit

In 1998, a group of scientists and engineers began an international and multidisciplinary project called the Global Consciousness Project (GCP). Data were collected from a network of RNGs located in about 70 major cities around the world. The purpose was to study the subtle influence of collective human consciousness on the physical world. Every second, each of the RNGs randomly generated 200 bits, and the sum of those bits were sent via the internet to a web server located in Princeton, New Jersey.

Peter Bancel and Roger Nelson observed that when major world events happened that focused collective attention, often by provoking an emotional response, the data collected by the GCP differed from chance expectation. Over the course of this nearly 20-year experiment, 500 events were identified (new year's celebrations, large terrorist attacks, the death of Pope John Paul II, for example), which provoked emotional reactions simultaneously in millions of people, overall generating a deviation from the chance-expected result with odds of over a trillion to one (Bancel and Nelson 2008; Bancel 2017).

Other interpretations of the data emerged and, in 2017 Peter Bancel proposed that the positive results obtained in that experiment were due, at least in part, to the psychic abilities of the experimenters; that is that people involved in the experiments, consciously or unconsciously, expected certain results and influenced, in an anomalous way, the behavior of the RNGs in the expected direction. Ongoing discussions continue to debate the best interpretations of the results of the GCP experiment.

Although some authors, such as Susan Blackmore (2003), have considered that the results obtained in these types of experiments were inconclusive, experiments and analyzes by many other researchers confirm the influence of human thought on the physical world (e.g., Dean Radin, Dick Bierman and Richard Broughton). These results challenge classical scientific conventions and warrant further research under the rigor of the scientific method, in order to possibly clarify the subject.

• 9 •

Willpower

THE EXPRESSION "WILLPOWER" IS ROOTED in the idea that, through our thoughts, we can successfully influence certain outcomes, and achieve good and useful things for ourselves and others. In the last few decades, several scientific researchers have explored this arca in humans and animals (Rhine 1971; Dutton and Williams 2009).

In the 1980s and 1990s, the French researchers Remi Chauvin and René Peoc'h performed experiments with rabbits, mice and chicks (Chauvin 1986; Peoc'h 1988, 1995, 2001). In the latter case, Peoc'h placed a small robot in the center of a rectangular arena. The robot moved randomly inside it, tracing a fuzzy trajectory across the whole of the interior of the rectangle. Then, on the outside of the rectangle, next to one side of the arena, the researcher placed a cage containing fifteen newly hatched chicks who could see what was happening on the inside of the rectangle, but could not enter it, nor move to any other side of the rectangle. Under these conditions, the robot made a trajectory similar to before, moving randomly around the whole rectangle.

Then, with the room in low light and with the same fifteen chicks in the same cage on one side of the rectangle, Peoc'h placed the robot in the center of the rectangle again but, this time, also placed a lit candle on top of the robot. The chicks could see the robot with the candle, but could not enter the rectangle, nor move to another side of the rectangle. This time, the robot moved much more along the side of the rectangle where the chicks were situated.

One way to interpret this outcome was that the chicks, wishing to be closer to the light or heat, emitted thoughts with sufficient strength to attract the robot to move toward them. There were some who replicated the experiment successfully (Fenwick 1996) and those who could not (Johnson 1989). Yet, overall experiments with animals have pointed in the same direction, such as the case of various experiments carried out by Rupert Sheldrake.

As previously mentioned, thought might be viewed as an energetic vibration that is transmitted through space in waves invisible to the human eye, somewhat analogous to electromagnetism. However, apparently, in the case of thought, similar poles attract and opposite poles repel each other. While with magnetism and electricity the positive pole attracts the negative pole and repels the positive pole, in the case of thoughts it appears that positive thoughts attract what is positive and repel the negative, and at the same time, negative thoughts attract what is negative and repel the positive.

A person who likes to drink a lot of alcohol prefers to spend time with others who also like to drink alcohol and not to be with people who only drink water and fruit juice. Those who only drink water and fruit juice like to be with those with similar tastes and not with those who prefer highly alcoholic drinks. In general, human beings like to be with those who think and act in similar ways to them and do not like to be with people who think and act in very different ways.

Accepting, hypothetically, the existence of life after physical death, it would make sense that things happen in a similar way. Or rather, a spiritual being already disconnected from its physical body which enjoyed strong alcoholic drinks will be attracted to human beings who also like that type of drink, and stay away from those who only drink water and juice.

In general terms, he who nurtures positive thoughts feels good near others who think in a similar way, attracting what is positive and repelling what is negative. Whenever that same person, on the other hand, transmits negative thoughts, he feels good near people who think in a similar way, attracting the negative and repelling what is positive. Thus, it is possible to generate spiritual fields of positivity and negativity.

Each one of us has our own free will, being able, in any moment, to opt to transmit positive or negative thoughts. When we think negatively, we surround ourselves with negative fields; things go badly, generating cycles of negativity. When we have positive thoughts, we surround ourselves with positive fields, facilitating constructive and useful activities (Walsh 2003).

Attention dispersed across several situations, animated by weak will, fed by thoughts of doubt and pessimism, will tend to prejudice the performance of useful actions and the achievement of merit-worthy goals. However, attention directed in a specific, useful direction, and animated by constructive thought and by strong and persistent will, enables the achievement of imagined actions and the concretization of beautiful goals. This, which the common human being learns through life experience, and which philosophers theorize, seems now to be demonstrated by several areas of science, including parapsychology. Maybe, in this way, people can become aware of the strength they have in themselves, of their great sensitivity and capacities for reasoning and achievement, liberating themselves from atrophying dependencies on third parties and intoxicating mystical practices.

Apparently, it is down to each person to define the meaning of their own life, to define who they really are, who they want to be, who they will be. They will only be able to be that when—using thought—they define it: when they resolve to do what is necessary for that end, using each moment of their life in the most appropriate way to evolve in the intended direction, to become who they envision themselves to be. For that, it is necessary for each person to wonder what, for them, is the purpose of life in general and to define the purpose of their own life.

However, it is not enough to define what to do. It is also necessary to concretize it. Everyone needs to define what they want to be and assume it. To be it. To be it intrinsically, even if they are not yet doing what is necessary. But not to wait for things to happen; to be it now, seeking to use all the resources available toward that end.

It seems that everything that each person is being is because they chose it, and because they created conditions to arrive where they are, to be what they are. It would be a mistake for people to believe that they are what someone wants them to be, what the others are giving them and/or result of what is happening around them. That which each person is was chosen by him—in the circumstances that he experienced—and not caused by third parties. The eventual induction implies an acceptance for the self. Who he now chooses to be, he will be, if he really wants it; and not what others want. So, each one must choose what he really wants to be, and be it, concentrating all his attention, all the strength of his positive though, all his available energy in that direction. Naturally, with pleasure, with love.

◆ 10 ◆

Neurosciences and Parapsychology

IN THE LAST HUNDRED YEARS, SCIENTIFIC EVOLUTION in the field of the neurosciences has been fantastic. With the help of increasingly more sophisticated equipment, scientists have made worthwhile developments which today allow us to understand neural activity, at the individual and collective level, from the cerebral cortex to the peripheral nervous system. However, there is still much to explain about physiological and pathological phenomena. Despite huge progress, there are still many aspects of the central nervous system with an unknown purpose, and still a lack of knowledge about the causes of several neurological disorders.

There seems to have been even less progress in knowledge related to the nature and capacities of consciousness. While accepting, through faith, the existence of an essential body of spiritual characteristics—our true self—humanity left behind the scientific study of such, as well as all of the related phenomena.

Since antiquity, there have been reports of human and animal experiences still unexplainable by science. But since the end of the 19th century, humans have given them some attention, leading to the formation of the scientific discipline calling itself "psychical research" in the form of the Society for Psychical Research, founded by scientists and scholars in London in 1882, and a few years later adopting the name "parapsychology," a term coined by German psychologist Max Dessoir. Parapsychology was further acknowledged as a scientific discipline by the American Association for the Advancement of Science in 1969, upon electing the Parapsychological Association as one of its affiliate members.

The Science of Spirit

This discipline uses the scientific method, albeit with the difficulties inherent in the study of phenomena which are often spontaneous, sometimes unconscious and, thus, difficult to reproduce on demand at specific dates and times in research laboratories. However, it involves phenomena that are more and more statistically proven, and it makes no sense to deny or ignore them. With further study, science takes on a wider, more holistic and global vision. And, for deeper scientific study of these phenomena and a more complete knowledge of our true selves, of the particles of energy that we are, perhaps an adjustment in the scientific method is necessary, accepting direct experiences with less objectivity.

Parapsychology was very isolated for several decades, maybe due to some of its researchers sometimes not being very rigorous in their methods, other times trying to impose their points of view or seeking to make money out of their work (devaluing the true and pure scientific spirit). But, with time, excellent researchers appeared, always using the rigor of the scientific method and publishing more and more the results of their work in scientific journals of quality. In recent decades, there has been a progressive collaboration between neuroscience and parapsychology, with researchers from the former trying scientifically to understand what goes on in the latter; getting involved in joint projects in ever greater numbers. Currently, research into parapsychology is also done by physicians, psychologists, nurses, physicists, mathematicians and scientists from other areas.

There have been studies of phenomena such as the mental perception of images not seen by others; as well as of the capacity to hear, smell or feel things that others cannot, those sensations relating to events taking place near or far, in the past, present or even the future. There have also been studies of the transmission of thought between two beings, near or far; the ability to speak about subjects that are unknown to the speaker, in some cases in languages also unknown to that individual; the ability to move objects near or far with no physical contact; and the ability to influence the behavior of third parties, near or far, by the power of thought.

Parapsychological phenomena were classified into psi-gamma, psi-kappa and psi-theta. The psi-gamma phenomena include telepathy or thought transmission—already dealt with in a previous chapter—and clairvoyance and precognition or premonition. Clairvoyance is the obtaining of information about an object or a current event without the use of the senses and without recourse to telepathy, since the information comes directly from an external physical source and not from the mind of another person. Precognition is the perception of information about future events that cannot be deduced from currently known data in the present.

Psi-kappa phenomena, telekinesis or psychokinesis, include macro-psychokinesis, micro-psychokinesis and bio-psychokinesis. Macro-psychokinesis—of which some examples have been presented already in this book—is the influence of thought over physical objects and systems, which can be directly observed via the senses—for example, the movement or distortion of objects. Large objects might be moved, even several of them at the same time, as happens in so-called cases of poltergeists or recurrent spontaneous psychokinesis (RSPK) and of hauntings. Both terms embrace less common types of psychokinetic phenomena with unknown origins, sometimes attributed to the presence of a certain person and/or spiritual beings.

The poltergeist event is generally centered on a certain person—often a child or adolescent—with high sensitivity, to whom are attributed characteristics of medium or "sensitive"; an accumulation of repressed anguish and rage is also frequently associated with these adolescents. Haunting is normally centered on a house or a place. Plenty of cases have been described of both phenomena, involving the appearance of non-retinal images, voices and strange sounds of apparently non-physical origin, as well as the movement of objects without the use of conventional physical forces. Since ancient times, people have attributed the origin of these phenomena to spiritual beings, identifying, for example, someone deceased with a relationship to the child or adolescent, or who lived in the house or interacted with its inhabitants. The presence of such a "sensitive" is what is thought to produce the phenomena; the "sensitive" is apparently a means or an agent conducive to the manifestations of energy yet not understood by science.

These situations have always piqued popular curiosity, but they were not studied by scientific researchers, and there remained a certain ignorance around them. Finally, as already stated, starting in the late 1960s, a small group of researchers from around the world dedicated themselves to the study of such phenomena despite the difficulty of framing them within the scientific method. Such spontaneous cases are, by their very nature, difficult to evoke or reproduce under experimental controls.

The English researchers Alan Gauld and Tony Cornell (1979) compiled 500 cases of poltergeists, analyzing their different characteristics and assessing the presence or absence of those characteristics in each case. More recently, James Houran and Rense Lange (2001), researchers in the Department of Psychiatry at the Southern Illinois University School of Medicine, published in their book, *Hauntings and Poltergeists: Multidisciplinary Perspectives*, a large review of the subject. In it, they reported many cases of poltergeists and hauntings, describing the socio-cultural context; advancing known explanations and the hypotheses that have grown up around them; presenting a discussion between those who highlighted certain fraudulent practices—remaining quite skeptical—and those who underlined the facts; pointing out the necessity of increasing scientific research which would permit the support and development of further knowledge. The theme is of great interest to the general public, when shown in cinema and on television. It is thrilling to see objects flying, marvelous or terrifying images; to hear strange noises from the dead, sometimes from deceased relatives.

Micro-psychokinesis—of which some examples have also already been presented in this book—is the influence of thought over random systems, such as throwing of dice, or random number generators, whose effects, on a small scale, may only be detected via statistical analysis. It has been researched, under the rigor of the scientific method, since 1934, at Duke University, but also in other universities, such as Princeton (Dunne and Jahn 2005).

Bio-psychokinesis, sometimes called direct mental interactions with living systems (DMILS), is the influence of thought over living organisms, like cell cultures, plants and animals, including humans, and encompassing distant healing and the detection of being observed by others (remote staring detection). Several researchers have studied mental influence over the growth of batches of seeds, compared to the growth of seeds in a control group, with statistically significant results (Creath and Schwartz 2004; Roney-Dougal 2002). Other scientists have analyzed the development of colonies of fungi and bacteria under the microscope (Nash 1982), comparing them to control groups, also finding statistically significant results. Bernard Grad (1976), of McGill University, in Canada, successfully studied the capacity to mentally influence scarring of surgical wounds in laboratory rats, compared to control groups.

Psi-theta phenomena include the study of life experiences outside the physical body, such as out-of-body experiences (OBE), near-death experiences (NDE), memories from supposed past lives, and instrumental transcommunication (Cardeña, Lynn and Krippner 2000; Fontana 2006; Irwin and Watt 2007; Roberts and Groome 2001). In the following chapters we will cover the research into these phenomena.

All the parapsychological phenomena involve a multiplicity of interacting and complex variables. But it is currently accepted that parapsychological abilities are normally distributed in the general population, existing to a greater or lesser degree in all individuals, although manifesting themselves more evidently in some people and only under certain circumstances. It is also accepted that parapsychological abilities may be developed through training and that skill in its use does not necessarily imply a heightened level of spirituality.

Perhaps an in-depth study of these phenomena would allow for a greater degree of knowledge as well as a competent and responsible use of these abilities, facilitating a holistic and unifying perspective and thus a way of becoming more complete. In this way, each human being could see themselves as a small particle of the universal whole while respecting the incredible degree of coherence and connectivity among all living beings or, even, between all the particles that exist in the universe, deeply and definitively interwoven (Andrade 2001; Bem and Honorton 1994; Braude 2003; Cetin 1999; Descamps et al. 1997; Goswami 2005; Green, Ooguri and Schwarz 2007; Greene 2004; Jahn et al. 1997; Radin 1997, 2006; Schwarz and Schwarz 2004; Sheldrake 2009).

◆ 11 ◆

Near-Death Experiences

M ANY PHYSICIANS AND PSYCHOLOGISTS have conducted stud- ies about near-death experiences (NDE), that is, on situations experienced by people who were close to death (or believed that they were), sometimes in a coma, sometimes even in cardiac arrest. This includes cases of people who suffered accidents or serious illness, in near-death situations; people who were resuscitated after being declared clinically dead for some minutes, hours or even days; and people who, in their last days of physical life, told what was happening to them.

In *Life After Life*, Raymond Moody discusses the study of life after the present physical life; rather, life after death. Moody is a graduate in medicine and was professor of philosophy of medicine at the University of North Carolina. He says: "I believe that all the great religions of man have many truths to tell us, and I believe that no one of us has all the answers to the deep and fundamental truths with which religion deals."

For several years, he studied more than a hundred and fifty cases of people who went through near-death experiences. In studying these situations, Moody, collecting all the data that was common to most of these cases, concluded:

A man is dying and, as he reaches the point of greatest physical distress, he hears himself pronounced dead by his doctor. He begins to hear an uncomfortable noise, a loud ringing or buzzing, and at the same time feels himself moving very rapidly through a long dark tunnel. After this, he suddenly finds himself outside of his own physical body, but still in the immediate physical environment, and he sees his own body from a distance, as though he is a spectator. He watches the resuscitation attempt from this unusual vantage point and is in a state of emotional upheaval.

After a while, he collects himself and becomes more accustomed to his odd

---

condition. He notices that he still has a "body," but one of a very different nature and with very different powers from the physical body he has left behind. Soon other things begin to happen. Others come to meet and to help him. He glimpses the spirits of relatives and friends who have already died, and a loving, warm spirit of a kind he has never encountered before—a being of light—appears before him. This being asks him a question, nonverbally, to make him evaluate his life and helps him along by showing him a panoramic, instantaneous playback of the major events of his life. At some point he finds himself approaching some sort of barrier or border, apparently representing the limit between earthly life and the next life. Yet, he finds that he must go back to the earth, that the time for his death has not yet come. At this point he resists, for by now he is taken up with his experiences in the afterlife and does not want to return. He is overwhelmed by intense feelings of joy, love, and peace. Despite his attitude, though, he somehow reunites with his physical body and lives.

Later he tries to tell others, but he has trouble doing so. In the first place, he can find no human words adequate to describe these unearthly episodes. He also finds that others scoff, so he stops telling other people. Still, the experience affects his life profoundly, especially his views about death and its relationship to life [Moody 1975].

It has been noted that it is rare that an individual describes all of these items; normally, only some are recalled. According to Greyson (2003), the most often described are the feelings of happiness, peace and love (85 percent), the perception of being outside one's physical body (70 percent) and the appearance of beings made of light (70 percent). Also, the order in which they are listed above, despite being the most common, can vary from person to person.

Researchers including Kenneth Ring (1980), Melvin Morse (1985, 1986, 1992), Justine Owens (1990), George Ritchie (1987, 1991), Peter Fenwick (2008) and Robert Kastenbaum (2011) described similar situations. Bruce Greyson (1983, 1993) identified sixteen items, considering that at least seven should be described to be considered a near-death experience, which has been defined as "a profound psychological event including transcendental and mystical elements, typically occurring to individuals close to death or in situations of intense physical or emotional danger" (Greyson 2000).

Some studies point to 10 percent to 23 percent of patients recovering from a cardiac arrest as describing a near-death experience (Greyson 2003; Klemenc-Ketis 2013; Parnia 2006; Schwaninger et al. 2002; Van Lommel 2001). The phenomenon, however, may also occur during meditative states (Beauregard, Courteman-che and Paquette 2009), following non-life-threatening situations (Charland-Verville et al. 2014), although at the time perceived as life-threatening by the subject (Gabbard and Twemlow 1991; Owens, Cook and Stevenson 1990) and sometimes following episodes of intense anxiety, existential crisis, grief or depression (Facco and Agrillo 2012).

Karlis Osis and Erlandur Haraldsson (1997) observed that the lack of oxygen to the brain is not the cause of near-death experiences—something which had been proposed by other authors—because pilots in the U.S. Air Force exposed to a lack of oxygen suffered only the visual kind of hallucinations, with geometric shapes. They did not report the classical signs of an NDE. Apart from this, other studies demonstrated an increase in oxygenation associated with near-death experiences (Parnia, Waller, Yeates and Fenwick 2001) or normal levels of oxygen (Klemenc-Ketis, Kersnik and Grmec 2010; Melvin, Morse and Donald 1985).

The majority of authors consider that people who experience near-death experiences are, generally, psychologically healthy. There are some cases of near-death experiences described by small children, who are presumably not influenced by philosophical concepts and transcendental expectations (Morse, Castillo, Venecia, Milstein and Tyler 1986).

The neurosurgeon Eben Alexander (2012) described in his best-seller *Proof of Heaven* his own experience of near death, after many years of prior skepticism about such experiences, when he had proposed that such situations were simply fantasies that occurred in cases of extreme stress. He now says that his NDE inspired him to help change the world for the better, calling for investment in scientific research, education and sharing of experiences of spiritual transformation.

When occurrences of near-death experiences are globally analyzed, the fact that a large number of people mention that their perspective about life is completely altered is impactful. They refer to the calm way in which they now face physical death; greater consideration for others; a strong sense of solidarity; a strengthened belief in an afterlife; a decrease in their interest in material things; an increase in self-confidence; a greater appreciation of natural phenomena; and greater respect for nature. These people began to live better and seek to improve conditions for others to do so (Greyson 2015; Groth-Marnat and Summers 1998; Van Lommel 2001).

The similarity between features of near-death experiences and cases of altered states of consciousness across cultures and over time is interesting (Belanti, Perera and Jagagheesan 2008; Kellehear 1993); similar experiences are described, as well, in several doctrines and religions, such as Tibetan Buddhism (Govinda 1959), yoga (Aurobindo 1970, 1976; Chaudhuri 1965), theosophy (Blavatsky 1979) and Christianity (Underhill 1955). Several authors consider that the existence of variability in the reports is not related to the experience itself but to the ability to understand and express such unusual experiences.

What happens after our physical death will always awaken the curiosity of humanity, which has speculated about this question from the beginning of its history. Maybe now the desire to really clarify the subject will be enough to support reputable and independent research, without preconceived ideas and taboos, and with the rigor of the scientific method.

◆ 12 ◆

Successive Lives

A S PREVIOUSLY MENTIONED, THERE ARE thousands of described cases of children who spontaneously report supposed past lives. It is common for them to cite names and events; they describe habits and places, things to which they could not have access, directly or indirectly. But it is also common for them to mention some incorrect information, which creates some doubt about these cases.

The research that some scientists have done in this area is praiseworthy, such as the work by Ian Stevenson, Erlendur Haraldsson, Antonia Mills, Tom Shroder, Jürgen Keil, Carol Bowman and Jim Tucker. Information was collected by specialists who studied the children and their families. The data was then cross-checked against data about the deceased, their families, their locations and the causes of their deaths.

Out of these researchers, I would like to highlight Stevenson for his pioneering, for the seriousness of his work, for his dedication to a life of research about the theme and for his notable results, which may come to decisively contribute to a change in the understanding of human presence on Earth. Ian Stevenson was born in 1918 in Montreal, Canada, and died in Charlottesville, Virginia, USA, in 2007. He was considered the best student in his medicine course in 1943, at McGill University, in the city of his birth. Having specialized in psychiatry, he worked in various North American universities, becoming director of the Department of Psychiatric Medicine at the Faculty of Medicine of the University of Virginia at 38 years, where he created the Division of Perception Studies (DoPS). This was, and continues to be, a research unit dedicated primarily to the study of cases of children who claim to have memories of previous life, as well as the study of near-death experiences.

Stevenson had been interested since his youth in parapsychological phenomena, which brought him, in 1960, to publish a study of 44 cases of individuals who presented memories of supposed past lives, which he collected from scientific literature. Right after this he travelled to India, where he studied 25 cases himself. Then, throughout his life, he travelled to other parts of the world where he studied and described many cases of children reporting supposed past lives, some of them presenting physical signs of this. At the age of 48, he published the bestseller *Twenty Cases Suggestive of Reincarnation*, illustrating cases in which he had been able to confirm the existence of the people described by the children he was studying. Or rather, he had been able to find factual data confirming the existence of the deceased person the child claimed to have been in a previous life.

In 1987, he published *Children Who Remember Previous Lives: A Question of Reincarnation*, and in 1997, *Where Reincarnation and Biology Intersect*. He has published fifteen books and hundreds of articles in scientific journals. Although having specialized in a topic which wasn't mainstream, he won the respect and admiration of academics, becoming a great figure in science. For Stevenson (1977), reincarnation "refers to the concept that human beings (and perhaps subhuman animals) consist of two separable components, a physical body and psychical entity or soul. At the death of physical body, the soul persists and, after a variable interval, becomes associated with a new physical body" (631). Stevenson also called the soul (the particle of universal energy) the "psychophore" in order to have a name without association with religious beliefs.

Stevenson's team investigated or analyzed around 3,000 cases of reported supposed past lives, across the five continents, in countries with a general belief in reincarnation, and in countries where the phenomenon is not generally accepted (Mills 1990; Stevenson 1980, 1983, 2003; Tucker 2007, 2008, 2013). They predominantly studied children, because there are more reported cases in childhood than in adulthood; but also because they considered children in general to be more reliable, namely when they knew things that they could not have learned because even the adults around them did not know.

The method consists of recording all the information mentioned by the child when he talks spontaneously about the supposed previous life, and also collecting any related information from the family, friends and neighbors. The researchers compare this with the information related to the existence of the person that the child says he has been before—who in many cases lived in a distant place or country—and hear the testimonies of families, friends and neighbors of that person, who may have known him directly or indirectly. All the information obtained is cross-referenced and all inconsistencies and discrepancies in the interviews and testimonies are analyzed.

Typically, these children verbalize information of a supposed past life; they begin to report these memories at the age of about 3 years and do so until they are 7 or 8 years old; they describe and recognize people, places, objects and events; they describe recent lives for which the interval between the physical death of the previous body and their own birth is from 1 to 2 years; they describe ordinary lives, but with 70 percent of deaths not by natural causes; sometimes they present behaviors related to a supposed previous life, namely phobias, aversions and attractions; they may have birthmarks or birth defects related to injuries demonstrably suffered in the previous life's body (Haraldsson 2000; Mills and Tucker 2015; Pasricha, Keil, Tucker and Stevenson 2005; Stevenson 2001; Tucker 2008).

Some children provide descriptions in a neutral manner, but many demonstrate a strong emotional involvement, crying and begging to return to their previous family. Others show hostility towards those who would have been their enemies or killers in that previous life (Tucker 2008). The majority of these children can remember the past life when questioned at any time. Quite often, these children involve themselves in games which seem to be related to their past lives, for example by simulating the profession of a past life.

In 68 percent of around 3,000 spontaneous cases registered by the University of Virginia it was possible to identify or confirm the previous personalities reported by the children. Those people really existed, which is notable, but the statements of each of these children are not generally entirely correct, the number of inconsistencies varying from case to case. Around 20 percent of these children report memories of events between lives (Tucker 2007). Some say that they remained for some time near the place where the previous personality lived or died; sometimes, they describe the funeral of that person and various events involving the family, after the death, the majority of which were confirmed.

Some studies assessing the psychological functioning of these children were carried out (Haraldsson 1995, 1997, 2003; Mills 2003; Tucker and Nidiffer 2014). Despite the results not being entirely consistent, it seems that the children who have memories of supposed past lives have good intellectual functioning. Although some show mild behavioral problems, generally they exhibit adaptive behavior, without signs of psychopathology; that is, it can be said that they are normal children.

According to Tucker (2008), detailed analysis of these cases seems to provide evidence that memories, emotions and even psychological traumas can, at least under some circumstances, carry over from one physical life to another. The processes involved in such a transfer of consciousness are still unknown and are worthy of investigation to allow further clarification.

Ian Stevenson (1993) researched 210 cases of children with birthmarks, such as areas without hair, wrinkled skin, under- or overpigmented areas of skin, scars resembling surgical incisions or other types of injury; and congenital defects, such as a hand almost without fingers: in one case it was reported and confirmed that the previous personality had placed his hand in the blades of a bailing machine and lost his fingers. In 1997, the same author published the book *Biology and Reincarnation: A Contribution to the Etiology of Birthmarks and Birth Defects*, in which he concluded that in 35 percent of confirmed cases of supposed past lives there existed birthmarks or birth defects which appeared to correspond to injuries or scars from the previous personality's life.

Some authors criticized the results of this kind of research, but the rigor of the scientific method which was always applied means that the possibility of fraud can be discarded. And some alternative explanations, such as paramnesia, cryptomnesia, extrasensory perception and inherited memory, were refuted, in a substantiated response by Stevenson himself and his followers. The existence of birthmarks, as well as recorded speech of children about supposed past lives without the family of the child having met the family of the previous personality (Keil and Tucker 2005; Schouten and Stevenson 1998), have strengthened the hypothesis of the survival of the soul after physical death, compatible with the theory of successive lives.

Adding this knowledge to the knowledge of spirituality, we may say that our true self is of spiritual nature that comes to Earth in successive experiences, animating different physical forms. The planet functions, therefore, as a kind of world-school, where we come to learn, evolving towards a progressive perfection, so we choose to come to Earth in many different situations, in accordance with what we most need to improve.

And in the period between two physical lives, what happens? Some lines of thought accept that the being which is liberated from the physical body, sooner or later, understands this and rises to its cosmic plane, according to its own spiritual evolution. More enlightened beings understand straight after their physical death, while the less evolved ones might stay connected—for days, months or years— to the events, people or belongings that they left, some thinking they are still physically alive, others understanding their actual state of being. Sooner or later, they do understand that their evolutionary trajectory must continue in another cosmic plane, where they meet, with satisfaction, other beings of a similar spiritual level, retrospectively analyzing their trajectory, and planning their future. From that time on, they stop spiritually disturbing those who are still physically on the planet.

It may be that, after they become completely enlightened, they opt to return physically to Earth or, eventually, to another world-school, to continue their learning in a new physical form of life. Or they may stay anchored in their cosmic plane—also called the astral plane—carrying out, from there, acts of spiritual support to those who are living their earthly lives and transmitting compatible thoughts. They may behave in a way commonly associated with angels or saints.

The known descriptions of these astral planes reveal another dimension, with beings without physical bodies, without defined form, without voice, but that are particles of energy which vibrate, analyze, reason, maintaining an extraordinary memory that includes everything of the past and maybe also having knowledge, at least partially, of the future. They live together with friend beings; intrinsic and absolute friends, by being at similar spiritual levels. Harmony, solidarity, complicity in objectives and attitudes reign between them.

They are a permanent consciousness that analyze past successes without glory or pride, and past failures without blame or humiliation. They clearly understand that things happened as, at the time, they were able to make them happen, and they maintain the constant possibility of being able to see everything, as if it were a film with many chapters of physical lives and with many intervals in between. A film in which nothing is left out, hidden or falsified, but where everything is recorded—from thoughts to actions—all the lives in world-schools as well as in astral planes.

As previously mentioned, there is a theory that, on returning to a world-school such as Earth, most beings choose the region of the world, their sex and their family where they feel they will find the best conditions to correct their errors of the past, to better develop their evolutionary trajectory. The choice of the parents will take into consideration a multifactorial context—from the spiritual level, and the experience of the current physical life, to the genetic and biological characteristics—which will end up influencing the individual. On the other hand, there is another theory that, on returning to the world-school, they are subject to forgetting all memories in order that, during their stay on the planet, they ignore everything from the past, while maintaining the essence of their evolutionary characteristics that they acquired in all their past lives. In this way, they can stay more focused on their learning.

Several authors refer to the possibility of accessing aspects of past lives when in states of relaxation, whether induced or spontaneous. In the astral planes, beings realize everything that is happening in the world-schools and what there is in the astral planes up to their own evolutionary level, but do not understand what is happening in the more evolved levels. In that way, the world-schools are places of learning between beings of different spiritual levels, while the astral worlds are places of reflection and organization, as well as activities for the good of the community, among beings of similar levels.

The impressive results in scientific research about past lives have come to be progressively accepted and today constitute an important base for the deepening of the study of life after death, as well as the study of successive physical lives.

◆ 13 ◆

Survival and Instrumental TransCommunication

HUMANS HAVE SOUGHT TO COMMUNICATE with the physically dead for a very long time. There are many descriptions of visual and audio messages left by those who supposedly exist in a dimension we cannot perceive with our five senses.

Traditionally, this contact was made by people with great sensitivity, considered capable of temporarily seeing, hearing, feeling, intuiting and/or embodying the expression of spiritual beings. They were called mediums for the fact that they were a medium through which the communication between the dead and the living was made. The difficulty of confirming the veracity of information transmitted via mediums, and the appearance of some frauds, made the existence of other means of communication with "beyond" desirable. When the first researchers heard the voice of a deceased person coming from the speaker of a radio, a new way of communication was noted.

Friedrich Jürgenson was a Swedish artist who dedicated himself to music and painting as well as to making films. He was a realist painter, mostly of portraits and landscapes, invited to paint Pope Pius XII, with whom he became friends. On 12 June 1959, when he was 56, he left a sound recorder outside his country house, to collect birdsong and the sounds of the forest. On listening back to the recording he was amazed to hear people's voices, even though the house was in an isolated place with no access for people to enter the property.

He decided to make further recordings, seeking to understand if these were voices of the dead. It was then that something happened that changed his life. In one of the recordings a voice he recognized appeared that said, "Friedel, can you hear me? It's your mother...." Friedel was a nickname given to him and used by his deceased mother. At that time, Jürgenson decided to go to the University of Freiburg, Germany, so the subject could be scientifically researched.

He also dedicated himself to the study of electronically recorded voices, live and via untuned radio equipment. In 1964, he published the book *Rösterna Från Rymden* (The Voices from Space). There followed other books on the subject, and some films. But he remained well known as an artist. He died in 1987, at the age of 84, leaving behind hundreds of recordings of the voices of apparently deceased people, and having predicted that this kind of message would one day be made through televisions with images associated with them, which did come to pass.

Instrumental Transcommunication (ITC) is a term introduced at the beginning of the 1980s by Ernst Senkowski, professor of experimental physics at the University of Mainz in Germany, for communication with that which is beyond (trans) our known physical reality, through technological devices. It consists of recordings of voices, images or texts—which cannot be transmitted by living beings—collected on sound recorders, radios, telephones, televisions, computers and fax machines. The designation of "electronic voice phenomena" (EVP) corresponds to a form of ITC which consists of hearing voices of unknown origin via an electronic device. There exist two kinds of EVP: one in which the voices are not heard by the people at the time it is recorded, but only when the recording is played back; the other in which the voices are audible via electronic equipment at the time in which they occur.

In 1936, the Californian Attila von Szalay was the first person to be able to record paranormal voices in sound recorders. In the middle of the 1950s, he joined Raymond Bayless, having collected much evidence of EVPs, and published the results of this research in the *Journal of the American Society for Physical Research* in 1959. The Latvian psychologist Konstantin Raudive was one of the researchers who worked with Jurgenson, resulting in the 1971 publication of the book *Breakthrough: An Amazing Experiment in Electronic Communication with the Dead*. Raudive thought that the voices came from deceased people who continued to exist spiritually in an alternative level to the physical world, which he called the "opposite world."

After this, all over the world, there appeared a growing number of reports of people who claimed to hear voices of the deceased via electronic equipment. There has also been some research published about the subject (Butler 2012; Cardoso 2010, 2012, 2017; Darnell 1979; Fontana 2006; Focher and Harsch 1995; MacRae 2005; Schaffer 1992; Senkowski 1995; Weisensale 1981). In a 2006 article, the university researcher David Fontana tried to inventory the advantages and difficulties of this kind of research, accepting that greater clarification about life after death will tend to expand the consciousness of human beings, giving them a more suitable idea of their position in the universe, but also allowing them a better alignment in the physical world in order to take full advantage of the opportunities for growth and evolution available in it.

The evidence of ITC can be tested by any person, with easily obtained equipment: a radio, a sound recorder and a microphone. With patience, dedication and openness, it is not hard to obtain results, which may be improved with experience and some more sophisticated equipment. The sounds and images obtained gain credibility by being captured via electronic instruments, without any apparent possibility of being influenced by humans. Above all, in the cases of long messages about subjects which are unknown to those present, and in the responses to improvised questions put by independent observers, instrumental transcommunication becomes more credible.

It is also an advantage that ITC permits a permanent record of the results obtained, which may be kept as proof. In the case of voices, they can be analyzed by highly qualified acoustic experts, who can distinguish characteristics that differ from human voices. Images can also be studied using the most sophisticated techniques used by the forensic police in some European countries and the USA.

The results obtained in this type of test, in which are compared two voice or image samples—one allegedly of a deceased person and another belonging to the same person but captured while he was still alive—are as reliable as the tests of voice and image recognition currently accepted by European and North American courts. Their margin of error is sometimes below 0.1 percent, although, in other cases, it varies between 5 percent and 40 percent. In some cases, the identity was confirmed in the samples; that is, the characteristics of the voices and the images of the individual were the same as when they were alive (Presi 2006).

Let us highlight some characteristics of EVP: the messages are complete phrases, not truncated at the beginning or end; the voice of the deceased person is commonly recognized by friends and family, as are expressions they commonly used in life; the messages are usually transmitted in the language of the listener, independent of their being in a country in which another language is used. EVP messages are not ambient sounds or radio signals (they do not include music, advertisements or news). Studies were carried out to determine if EVP messages were intercepted radio signals, of voices or other unrecognized sounds. MacRae (2005) collected EVP messages in a secure room shielded against radio frequency signals, sound signals or electric signals. In another study, a radio and a recorder were placed in a padded box, which was then buried. The recorder could not record radio programs but recorded EVP messages which appeared out of the noise produced by the radio (Weisensale 1981).

ITC is a legitimate form of studying life after death, but it does not seem suitable to satisfy personal curiosity or to ask for favors from spiritual entities, not taking responsibility for what is our duty to do. Some scientists have thought that the evidence of survival presented by ITC is not convincing. It seems advisable for there to be a deepening of its study, following all scientific standards in the experiments to ensure honesty and transparency in the processes, but it also seems necessary to be open to discard some constrains and old paradigms. It would even be defensible to prioritize the study of the conditions which allow the communication with, above all, very evolved beings, who may leave enlightening and useful messages, encouraging humanity to better realize its full potential.

Ernst Senkowski, professor of experimental physics and author of the book *Instrumental Transcommunication: Dialogue with the Unknown*, says that we should consider all the objective facts and subjective experiences which concern the most important of questions: survival. We will probably never find "scientific proof" in such a reductive system, but there is more than enough "evidence," that should lead us to search new definitions of "proof," in the context of new paradigms (Cardoso 2010). The priest and professor of theology François Brune, member of the research committee of IANDS, the International Association for Near-Death Studies, claims: "Communications received via instrumental transcommunication are very important since they may be tested, and possibly accomplished, by anyone[...]. Science must accept its limits and research paranormal phenomena, even if for that to happen some established paradigms are overtaken. It must foresee the existence of other paradigms, be ready to formulate other theories and free itself from some constraints."

◆ 14 ◆

Astral Body

THE VAST MAJORITY OF HUMANITY ACCEPTS the existence of
something more than the physical body. Some speak of the
soul, others of the spirit. Some believe it to be eternal, others not.
Some describe just one non-physical structure, others describe two,
three, five or more. But there is a certain consensus that our essential
nature is not physical and, therefore, cannot be seen, heard, smelled
or touched. It is intelligence, life, creative and constructive power.

Several pre–Christian doctrines—for example in India, China
and Egypt—defended the existence of a subtle body, with a form
similar to the human body, made of an ethereal substance although
still not identifiable by the human eye. The etheric double, astral
body and vital body are some of the names still used, above all in
spiritualist circles (Besant 1917; Blavatsky 1979; Leadbeater 1902).
According to them, the spirit hangs over the astral body and the
physical body, animating them, being the vibration responsible for
the generation and emission of thought. The brain decodes and
interprets the thoughts which are emitted by the spirit and transmitted through the astral body, which in turn registers the memories of
the thoughts.

The astral body is "fluidic," molded by the spirit, apparently with
characteristics marked by its evolutionary level, in which memories
of the recent, distant or very distant past are stored, marking emotional, intellectual and even organic tendencies. It can be seen by
some people in a form similar to the physical body, but it may also
be reshaped by the spirit into other forms, once it is free of the physical body.

The Science of Spirit

"Silver cord" is the name given to the connection between the spirit, the astral body and the physical body, which is revealed when the bodies separate. It is called the *sutratma* in the East and golden vessel in the Bible. Some say it is linked to the heart, others that it is linked to the heart and the brain and still others that it connects these two structures and the solar plexus. It is a fine ethereal thread, a filament of energy, which is said to have the capacity to stretch infinitely through the universe, permitting the astral body to be far from the physical body. Breaking it means death of the physical body.

According to this theory, in the waking state, the various constituent bodies of the human are concentric, with the silver cord being invisible. During sleep, the physical body and the others separate, thus revealing the silver cord, although only visible to a very small number of people with visual acuity far higher than the normal (Andrew 1994; Besant and Leadbeater 1901; Blackmore 1993; Collerton, Perry and McKeith 2005; Morales 2004). In out-of-body experiences, sometimes called unfolding or astral projections, the silver cord can be seen while the consciousness leaves the physical body. These experiences can supposedly be trained by transcendental meditation—of which Hornell Hart (1954), of Duke University in North Carolina seems to have been the pioneer researcher—but can also occur spontaneously.

According to Charles T. Tart, retired professor of psychology at the University of California, Davis, the individual realizes that he is occupying a different space from his physical body, able to observe it from the outside. If he wants, he can move at the speed of his thoughts, wherever he wants to go, stretching, without any difficulty, the silver cord. This theory explains the phenomenon called bilocation, in which the presence of a person in two places is noted at the same time, which has happened with various figures beatified by the Catholic Church, such as António of Padua and Francisco Xavier. Thus it is established the possibility of being apart from the physical body, moving spiritually to another place, the astral body being seen by those with ability.

For spiritualists who defend this theory, it is through the astral body and the silver cord that life energy flows from our true self to our physical body. When this energy stops being transmitted, the silver cord breaks and causes physical death. The case of deep coma, with brain death, is explained by the partial breaking of the cord, breaking the filaments that connect to the brain, while the filaments that are connected to the heart stay intact.

When humans feel, for example, a strong emotion, the spirit—if not duly prepared to control itself and remain strongly connected to thoughts that are positive, constructive and high—may be shifted, squeezed and even disturbed. In this situation, the astral body contracts, diminishing the energy flow to the physical body. In a severe occurrence and if repeated often, physical and/or mental illness may appear in the more affected organ or organs.

Many spiritualists believe that the majority of illnesses are caused by the weakening of the spirit which, when it becomes discouraged, when it lessens in strength, transmits less life energy to the physical body. Many illnesses can thus begin in the weakening of thought and spirit, which causes lower levels of life energy to reach the astral body and physical body, allowing illness to appear.

As mentioned, there have been reports of radiations emitted by the physical bodies of various kingdoms in nature, notably in good human beings, who appear and are portrayed with an aura of light colors, sometimes silver or gold. Normally these radiations are invisible to the human eye, but they can be seen by beings who are clairvoyant mediums and by many animals. Kirliangraphy currently allows the physical detection of at least some of these radiations emitted by animals and plants.

Each aura has its own unmistakable frequency, but its color can change—especially in humans—according to the person's physical health, emotional state and kind of thoughts. Normally, light colors are compatible with good states of physical and mental health, as well as positive, constructive and high thoughts. On the contrary, dark colors are associated with cases of illness and negative thoughts (Alvarado and Zingrone 1994; Andrews 1994; Kilner 1993;

Leadbetter 1995). Through the study of auras, the kind of thoughts that animate a person may be seen. Maybe in the future it will be possible to detect illness early through the analysis of aura.

These are speculative ideas, still not accepted by the majority of scientists, who consider them not to be scientifically proven.

◆ 15 ◆

Regression and Progression

B RIAN WEISS WAS TRAINED IN MEDICINE at Yale University and
did his internship in psychiatry at the Bellevue Medical Center
of New York University (NYU). He was professor in the department
of psychiatry at the University of Miami and worked in the department of psychiatry of Mount Sinai Medical Center, of which he is
chairman emeritus.

One day, in 1980, during a regression therapy session, one of his
patients began to remember, with incredible precision, situations
which she said she had lived in past lives, from the second millennium
before Christ until the middle of the 20th century. Weiss and some of
his colleagues studied the experiences reported by the woman, experiences that she could not have known in her current lifetime, check-
ing the veracity of some of the facts she had recounted. This episode
changed the life of this skeptical psychiatrist, who decided to dedicate
himself to the study of such situations, studying more than four thousand cases of patients who described past lives, many of them while
under hypnosis. He became the author of bestsellers in which he
described his clinical experiences, such as "Many Lives, Many Masters" (1988), "Through Time into Healing" (1993), "Only Love Is Real"
(1997) and "Same Soul, Many Bodies" (2004).

Brian Weiss believes that, when better studied, this situation
will forever change the way that life is generally perceived. But there
exist few published scientific articles about this theme, despite the
many other physicians and psychologists who use what is called past
life regressive therapy (PLRT) or past life therapy (PLT), which consists of "an intuitive and symbolic form of regression therapy, using

mental imagery, and dealing with the unconscious. It accesses and revives scenes which seem to be from the past or future to make changes in the client's perspective of the present" (Clark 1995, 4).

Following some controversy that the use of hypnosis may lead the therapist to induce, albeit involuntarily, the client to imagine himself in a previous life (Spanos et al. 1991; Stevenson 1994), more recently a light altered state of consciousness has begun to be used, keeping the client aware of what is going on and thus able to decide to stop a session when he wants. The questions should be put in a very open manner, avoiding leading the client's answers. An effective way of doing this is for the therapist simply to ask the patient to return to the cause or causes of the problem which affects him currently. According to several authors—including Clark (1995), Freedman (2002), Solovitch and Henricot (1992)—PLRT allows for quick and effective treatment of a wide variety of problems, including migraine, phobias, difficulties in relating to others, depression, insomnia, weight problems and asthma. In this way, a considerable number of psychiatrist and psychologists use regressive therapy, making their patients—in a state of deep relaxation—return to their first years of life, to their intrauterine life, and beyond to supposed past lives (Barbeau et al. 2005; Bowman 1998; Dethlefsen 1976; Lucas 1993; Simões 2003; Wamback 1978).

During the therapeutic process, the patients may express strong emotions, as if they are effectively re-experiencing the scenes which they describe. Sometimes, they cry tears of sadness or happiness, grimace or express joy or contort their bodies in pain (Woolger 1988). But it became clear that, for the therapy to succeed, neither the therapist nor the patient needs to believe that those experiences correspond to scenes genuinely lived by another body in a distant or recent past; that is, they don't need to believe in the theory of successive lives.

For the therapeutic process to work all that is needed is a careful association between the "memory" being "relived" by the patient and the problems in his present life, the elimination of these being possible through seeing the connection and the removal of this connection (Clark 1997). The majority of past life therapists believe that the images recounted by patients are a combination of real past lives, metaphors and fantasies. Some researchers analyze occurrences, places and details obtained through regression therapy, confirming historical truths in many and inaccuracies in others (Currie 1998). However, the accuracy of some details recounted by some people is impressive, taking into account that they have never studied or had any connections with things of centuries past.

For example, Linda Tarazi (1997), psychotherapist and researcher, analyzed the case of one of her American clients (L.D.), who regressed back to the life of a Spanish woman named Antonia in the late 16th century. During sessions, Tarazi compiled detailed historical data, which she could only confirm later, upon consulting centuries-old municipal records from the city of Cuenca, Spain, and other old Spanish archives. These resources weren't available to L.D., since she could not speak Spanish, nor had she ever been in Spain. Several times, the historical information supplied by L.D. as Antonia was initially considered wrong, but later validated, after detailed study of the official archival records in Spain. Some examples of the verified information included "old Spanish shipping laws governing trade to the Indies: details about various types of ships used in Mediterranean and Atlantic Ocean at that time; names of priests executed in 1581 and 1582 and method of their execution; [...] the name of eight friends of Antonia living in Cuenca, Spain, in the late 1500s (these names were found in Inquisition records and/or the Municipal and Diocesan Archives)" (Bettis 1998, 60–61).

In the practice of regression therapy, some patients began to describe scenes from future lives, from a few days or weeks ahead, or even months, decades or centuries. That is, these patients, instead of regressing, were progressing in time. The therapeutic value of these cases has also been of use sometimes, although the therapist must be very careful, alerting the patient to the possibility of the content being merely imaginary, or projections of subconscious desires.

To study progression, some researchers (Snow and Wambach 1989; Weiss 2004) instructed volunteers under hypnosis to advance through time focusing on a specific theme, arriving at a certain time period in the future. After some weeks or months, the experiment was repeated and the volunteers were asked to progress again to the same time period and on the same theme. They saw that the scenarios were not the same, being slightly better or worse.

Saving this data, they waited for time to pass, until the events described in these scenarios occurred and, then, asked the volunteers what, after all, had happened. The answers pointed to one of the scenarios previously referred to. In the worst-case scenario, many of the volunteers admitted to not having given much value to the progression experiments because foreseen things had happened, and they hadn't put much effort into getting things to go better. While in the cases in which one of the better scenarios foreseen had happened, many of the volunteers had taken the initiative of making sure, bearing in mind the scenarios they had experienced during the progressions, that they took care for things to go better.

Thus, the future scenarios described by the patient were possibilities that might happen or not, depending on the decisions made by the patient. According to Weiss (2004), "Our *individual* immediate futures [...] depend to a large extent [...] on our choices and actions in the present. Our long-term futures—our *collective* futures, the future of our planet [...]—depend on the cumulative decisions of all people" (214).

These studies on progression to the future seem to confirm the spiritual belief that chance does not exist; our present being the fruit of our past decisions and our future being the result of that which we want and build by our efforts. According to this conception, every time we make choices, we are molding our future, whether in individual or collective terms. When we become aware of this, we tend to face the future in a truly responsible way, assuming responsibility for our actions and using our free will appropriately, in a useful way for ourselves and for others. In this way, we create conditions for ourselves to progress and to contribute towards the general progression of humanity.

Free will is the ability to do or not to do any act, or rather, the freedom each human has to act using his reason, according to his higher interests or, on the contrary, according to his tendencies. It is, then, a characteristic controlled by will and, when well used, orientated by reason. It is the power which the human has, as opposed, apparently, to all other animals, to self-determine, that is, to choose his path independently of his own tendencies, outside influences and environmental circumstances in general. It is his own will which behaves as a judge or referee in decision making.

It is accepted, then, that no object, no value, no necessity (physical, metaphysical or moral) can impose itself on human choice. The human being does not need, nor does he have to be commanded by, anything or anyone, having the consciousness of his own responsibility in deciding his present and his future. Using free will, the individual has the power to construct his own path, through his thoughts and through his actions. Through accumulated experiences, he strengthens his conviction that his luck comes from his own capacity to decide his path. Thus, he can at any moment change the direction of his life.

Making selfish or perverse decisions, he is naturally complicating his future with disorientation and suffering, which along with indolence, indifference and negligence, slow down his natural evolutionary progress. Evolution takes place when the individual, with full use of his free will, uses reason and directs his will, thinking constructively and acting in tune with universal laws, according to his highest interests, which bring him closer to the highest interests of others and, then, the whole. The individual continues to correct his evolutionary trajectory, not because he is obliged to, but freely, because that option is the one which brings him the deepest pleasure of personal realization, of contributing to the whole and progressive integration into this.

Education should therefore not be repressive or too normative, but mostly orientating, directed towards universal values and responsibility in the direction of development of firm conviction in one's own capacity to choose thoughts, select words and decide upon actions. As he evolves, the human being gets less excited by material pleasure in things and automatically abandons actions which his conscience censures. The more he stays attentive and diligent in correcting his path, the more progress he makes, acquiring wisdom and developing his capacity to control ever better his thoughts and actions, in the fine tuning of his free will.

In this way, it is advisable for each individual, from time to time, to ponder on whether he has or has not acted in accord with his higher interests—which also means acting in the higher interests of others—and in how to manage to control himself rationally, to appropriately use his free will and achieve greater material and spiritual success. In this exercise, some questions assume primordial importance. It is pertinent to analyze his capacity in maintaining thoughts oriented positively to his advantage and that of others close to him. It is important to consider the development of the strength of will and if this has been applied in a positive way.

It is worth examining if he has maintained emotional balance, avoiding all and any lack of control (verbal, attitudes and even thoughts). It is essential to appreciate fulfillment of family and professional responsibilities and, complementary to this, the kind of language used, the diet, how free time is spent and even the management of sleeping hours. It is worth considering the level of self-confidence and the frequency and degree of assumption of responsibilities. It is also good to establish up to what point the habit has been adopted of making decisions only after giving them due ponderation and having achieved a beneficial interior serenity.

Analyzing his ability to maintain good humor, especially in difficult moments, must not be forgotten. It is also advantageous to check his level of respect for peers, level of tolerance, words and actions used in situations of disagreement. It is also useful to see how often, on the other hand, he does to others what he would like them to do to himself, as well as his availability to be useful without asking for anything in return. Further, it is pertinent to analyze his ability to peaceably move away from hostile, defamatory or in any way undesirable environments, and to forget about them.

Consider this opportune thought of Albert Einstein:

But the scientist is possessed by the sense of universal causation. The future, to him, is every whit as necessary and determined as the past. There is nothing divine about morality, it is a purely human affair. His religious feeling takes the form of a rapturous amazement at the harmony of natural law, which reveals an intelligence of such superiority that, compared with it, all the systematic thinking and acting of human beings is an utterly insignificant reflection. This feeling is the guiding principle of his life and work, in so far as he succeeds in keeping himself from the shackles of selfish desire [2007, 29].

• 16 •

Mediumship

I N THE BEAUTIFUL FILM *THE SIXTH SENSE* by M. Night Shyamalan, two aspects stand out: the outstanding performances of Bruce Willis and, above all, of little Haley Joel Osment, and a screenplay that can be understood as seeking reality rather than fiction. Haley Joel, at about 10 years of age, brilliantly interpreted the difficult role of a child gifted with mediumship.

The director explores the theme of the sixth sense, or extrasensory perception, or mediumship, in an intelligent way. It is interesting to see a certain absence of sensationalism, a concern with treating the theme with some seriousness, in search of what might be real and provoking a scary feeling here and there in the spectator. As the director and writer of the film himself said, the film is "reality based fright. It comes from the fears of real people, real children and real adults, fears of loss, the unknown, of having a sixth sense about what lies beyond and fears of not understanding those intuitions."

The Sixth Sense is one of those films that make us think about various things: the continuity of existence of the spirit beyond physical death; the possibility of the spirit remaining in the atmosphere of the Earth, trying to interfere in the activity of physically living beings; the hypothesis that such spirits are able to see themselves and show themselves to others with a "fluidic" body (many times called astral body), very similar to the one they inhabited while alive; the possibility of some humans seeing and/or hearing these beings, making contact with them through thought or even verbal expression.

And more: the possibility of seeing images or hearing sounds, whether pleasant or unpleasant; the capacity of those who can see or hear to be impressed or influenced, as well as the capacity to remain calm, whatever happens; the possibility of feeling spiritual beings through mere intuition or various physical sensations, without seeing or hearing, or even smelling them. The ability to attract or tune in to these beings or repel them through the power of thought. Hence, the possibility of less evolved spiritual beings being able to harm people and very evolved spiritual beings being able to help them. Also the capacity, through negative thoughts, of human beings to attract and tune in to what is negative and, through positive and/or constructive thoughts, attract and tune in to what is positive. What may constitute the key to truly responsible human behavior—the understanding that, through thought, the human being opts to reconnect himself to what is or is not important to him.

Some of these forms of mediumship have been approached in other films such as *Ghost, City of Angels, What Dreams May Come, The Exorcist, Poltergeist,* and *Hereafter.*

Many people believe in the existence of a sensitivity to that which is non-matter, or rather, beyond what the five senses can detect, although it is in some way related to them. In the past, it was believed to be an ability that just some people possessed but, currently, many authors believe that it exists in all people in some innate form, although more in some than others. Some people have a specific type of mediumship more developed (for example, just hearing the spirit), while others have several types of well-developed mediumship (for instance, sensing, hearing and seeing the spirit). It is also believed that such skills can be developed with effort. In 1991, Haraldsson and Houtkooper published the results of a study carried out in 13 European countries and in the U.S., involving 18,607 people, who were asked if they had ever felt as if they were in contact with someone deceased; 25 percent of the responders answered positively.

This type of sensitivity is called mediumship. The most common skill may be intuitive mediumship, but others are clairvoyance (seeing), clairaudience (hearing) and clairalience (smelling), telepathy, xenoglossy, psychography, xenography and channeling mediumship

(Moreira-Almeida 2004). Clairvoyance is the relatively common ability to visualize images not directly related to material bodies. It is copiously described, from banal, quotidian situations to visions promoted by religions, such as in the cases of Lourdes and Fátima (Cheroux et al. 2004; Collerton et al. 2005; Houran and Lange 2001; Kastenbaum 1988).

Xenoglossia is the rare ability to speak in foreign languages which are unknown to the speaker (Stevenson 1976). Psychography is the similarly rare ability to write about a subject about which the writer knows nothing, picking up a pen and letting his hand write, often with eyes shut (Rocha et al. 2014)—as was the case of Fernando Pessoa—sometimes with handwriting similar to the communicating entity (Lancastre 1981). Xenography is the even rarer ability to write in a foreign language unknown to the writer.

There are some mediums who, under certain conditions, draw or paint with skill, sometimes with their eyes shut, sometimes faithful copies of famous works. There are also mediums who, under certain conditions, recite poetry by heart, without knowing the poetry previously. In both cases, the mediums normally have no abilities in those areas, and have never learned them.

In channeling mediumship, the medium allows their physical body to be temporarily controlled by a spiritual being, being able to assume the personality of the latter, its tone of voice, the use of words or phrases they commonly used in life, their sense of humor and even mannerisms (Braude 2003). It is as if, for a few minutes, the human being becomes the puppet of a spiritual being.

Intuitive mediumship is the ability to receive ideas from third parties, whether unconsciously, as appears to happen with most people, or consciously, which can be done through study and training. Sometimes perfectly regular people suddenly, think, say and do things that have nothing to do with their way of thinking and which they cannot explain. Suddenly, they have a certain thought which induces them to say and/or do something that they had never thought of before, and do it without considering the situation in which they find themselves. Only some days, weeks or months later, do they admit that they lost control of themselves and took attitudes that didn't match their own will, feelings or most deeply held convictions. They recognize, then, that—because of some uncontrolled bad intuition they had felt—they might have badly hurt someone due to their lack of control, often someone who was very dear to them.

For a long time, the characteristics of mediumship in the human have been used for diverse mystical practices, creating many concepts around them, some taboos and various doctrines and religions. These allow fantasies around beings who are more developed mediums, sometimes being considered possessed and even condemned to death, other times believed to be vehicles for a divine mission and having some of their experiences called miraculous. Unfortunately, much business has been done around mediumship, and these misconceptions, taboos, doctrines and so-called miracles are often designed to exploit the ignorance of people. Only since the end of the 19th century has science begun to seriously study mediumship, seeking to distinguish between the true and false, exploring relationships of cause and effect and creating conditions for replicability (Bartolomei et al. 2004; Carpenter 2012; Kelly and Arcangel 2011; Radin 1997; Rhine and Brier 1984).

This subject has been studied by a number of researchers in the last century (e.g., Beischel, Bocuzzi et al. 2015; Delorme et al. 2013; Jensen and Cardeña 2009; Rock 2014; Schwartz 2002). In diverse situations, it was observed under highly controlled conditions that mediums could supply accurate information about deceased personalities unknown to them. This information may involve details about the circumstances of their physical death, or intimate names or incidents known only by a few close relatives of the communicating deceased personality.

Several researchers claim that the accurate and specific information supplied by mediums might be explained solely by extrasensory perception. Mediums may, for example, obtain the information telepathically (often unconsciously) through the people who seek them out for communication with the dead. Although this explanation may apply in some situations, it is unlikely when the communicating personality provides information which is accurate but unknown to the "sitter"—the person who had a close relationship with the deceased and who resorts to a medium to obtain information and/ or establish contact with the same—and, above all, when there is no living sitter with knowledge of the deceased personality. There are cases in which a deceased personality who is unknown to the medium and the sitters appears spontaneously and provides specific details which can be seen later to be accurate. A "drop in" communication—a casual visit, without previous warning—is considered by some authors a strong evidence for the hypothesis of life after physical death (Stevenson 1970, 1973; Rocha et al. 2014).

The majority of scientists who research mediumship believe that conventional explanations, such as unconscious mental activity and fraud, might explain only some of the observed cases. Thus, they propose that extrasensory perception or life after physical death are more viable hypotheses than more mundane explanations (Almeder 1992; Beischel 2007; Beischel et al. 2015; Bem 2005; Braude 2003; Kelly 2010; Moreira-Almeida 2012). To avoid any bias, recent studies on mediumship have followed a triple-blind protocol, in which no participants in the study—medium, sitter and researcher—possess information about the deceased person to be contacted, nor do they have a way of obtaining that information by conventional means.

For example, in a study by Beischel and Schwartz (2007) eight sitters were selected, four of whom had experienced the death of a parent and four of whom had experienced the death of a colleague or friend. A first researcher, who had no contact with the medium, collected information specific to the deceased, regarding the following characteristics: age, physical appearance, description of personality, hobbies/activities and cause of death. The four deceased parents were paired with the four deceased friends, each being different in the characteristics mentioned. The medium did not know the identity of the sitters nor the deceased (blind condition 1), having only the first name of the deceased indicated to them.

A second researcher, who interacted with the medium as a way of reproducing a conventional reading by putting questions to the medium, also did not know the identity of the sitters nor the deceased (blind condition 2). This strategy is called "proxy sitter," where the person who desires communication with the deceased loved one is not physically present in the session and in his place is a representative, with no knowledge about the deceased. This method has the advantage of eliminating the sitter as a source of information either via sensory cues or via telepathy.

The sitter had to rate two transcriptions (the medium's reading formatted into an item list), one relating to the deceased person that they knew (reading intended for him), and another related to a stranger (the control reading), not knowing which was which (blind condition 3). The sitter ranked each reading from 0 (no correct information) to 6 (excellent reading, with much information, practically all correct) and selected that which applied more to the deceased person that they knew (intended reading). The sitters gave significantly higher scores to the readings intended for them (mean = 3.6) compared to the control readings (mean = 1.9). Three mediums obtained very high averages for their communications (from 5 to 5.5), and two obtained moderate results (3.5). In 81 percent of cases, the sitters correctly selected the reading intended for them.

Recognizing thoughts as vibrating waves which cross the universe, emitted by human beings and other animals (May, Utts, Humphrey, Luke, Frivold and Trask 1990; Schmidt, Schneider et al. 2004; Sheldrake 2004), as well as by spiritual beings who have already left their physical bodies, makes us aware of our ability to receive those thoughts, allowing them, or not, to influence our lives. People with greater sensitivity will receive more, and better, thoughts that traverse the universe, something which is enriching in allowing a better understanding of what is happening. What is bad is if the individual does not know how to separate his own thoughts from those which reach him from elsewhere, feeding his own confusion, and does not know how to defend himself from what is negative, ending up being disturbed, probably because the thoughts echo his own weaknesses.

As sensitivity develops, the human being senses more and more what is happening around him. In the beginning, this development is somewhat uncontrolled and done with little consciousness. But, with time, the being can distinguish between what he senses from the exterior and what are his own thoughts; and can train the latter in order that he stays on the right path for his own higher interests.

In this way, it would be advantageous for all of us to seek to know ourselves better; for this we can use the exercises of relaxation and meditation, as well as introspective reflection which allow us to grow our knowledge of ourselves, including our sensitivity and abilities to use universal energy. A good daily exercise to do is described in the chapter entitled "Discernment." It allows us to use our sensitivity constructively to serve ourselves and to serve others, in a balanced life. In this way, we progressively feel better.

And we evolve, until we become capable of watching an argument without getting involved in it, always having constructive thoughts, calmly seeking an intelligent, balanced, fair and worthy solution for all. Until we are conscious of our sensitivity, but don't let ourselves be disturbed anymore by the negative thoughts which reach us—regardless of their source—winning the right to live serenely, in spiritual peace, and radiating that peace all around us. We understand that our sensitivity is, in fact, an instrument to serve us and, through us, to serve (as a gift to) others.

• 17 •

Intuition

EVERYONE LIKES TO HAVE GOOD IDEAS, to feel inspired, to feel good intuitions flow through them. In the middle of serious problems or in a reflective mood, or even when we wake up in the middle of the night, we all find pleasure in being endowed with ideas which contribute towards the resolution of problems, which open up new paths, which help us to live better or, indirectly, to improve the lives of those around us.

Intuition is the capacity of direct and immediate knowledge, without recourse to reasoning or the sensory organs. For the professor of psychology and psychiatry at the universities of Zurich and Basel, Carl Gustav Jung (1971), it is a psychological function, by virtue of which we have a tendency to seek the origins of things and we sense their evolution or transformation. It is considered a sixth sense, through which we spontaneously and automatically feel what attitude to take, which path to follow, what decision to make or action to take. It could be considered a form of mediumship.

It seems to be fairly common, although it varies in intensity and frequency from individual to individual and in each individual. A person's intuition varies according to diverse circumstances, like the type of thoughts that he has, the environment in which he finds himself and his capacity to be more or less influenced by that environment. A depressed person, for example, seems to have greater difficulty in intuiting than a person experiencing a psychologically strong moment. And, while that person seems to have an easier time in intuiting positive or favorable things, probably by emitting thoughts of that kind, negative intuitions predominate in the depressed person.

The person who trusts too much in his intuitions ends up by finding inaccuracies and incongruities, for which it is advisable that the necessary confidence be complemented with some thoughtfulness in the analysis of the intuitions, and some moderation in his tendency to use them. Jung proposed screening our intuitions, simultaneously with feeling, emotion and reason, only trusting in the situation if all agreed.

It is normal for people to say that in some situations or environments—such as at home or in contact with nature—they feel more likely to show intuitive abilities; while in other situations or environments—for example, of great confusion or depravity—they have a tendency to intuit less and or to intuit disagreeable things. Everything indicates that people with stronger personalities have a greater capacity to be less affected by their environment. But various authors defend the possibility that this capacity can be developed, it being possible to learn to place thought in a way that one can intuit beautiful things, even when surrounded by adverse circumstances.

Also, it appears that the intuitive ability itself can be developed. Some researchers advise that we start by freeing our imagination through simple reproductions of what we already know. Then, creative imagination allows us to surpass the limits of space and time. To develop our imagination, it appears to be useful for us to bear in mind some details which pass unnoticed to many people, but which may be the starting point for the creative imagination and, later, for intuition. Good concentration seems to facilitate a developed consciousness of things, opening us up to subtle impressions, previously undetected. And those impressions may originate within us as much as they may come from the material or immaterial exterior.

On the other hand, it also seems useful to use a memory as complete as possible, reaching all levels of consciousness and, according to some authors, be able to extend to the far reaches of universal knowledge, which Jung called "the collective unconscious." Such authors consider that such knowledge may not have been gained directly by us or may have been gained in other earthly lives, but to which we may have access only because of our availability for such, and our required persistence (Bierman and Scholte 2002; Kagan 2002; Segalowitz 2007).

The expansion of consciousness can minimize some obstacles, allowing us to embrace another dimension, with the growing assumption of total responsibility for our past, present and future actions, as well as, obviously, the thoughts which feed them. Intuition must be, then, just a window, or a set of windows, which broaden the narrow horizons in which we move, allowing us to be more responsible and more complete. Apparently, it is fundamental to be able to achieve a purity of intentions and systematically maintain positive thought, eliminating emotional negativity. Thus, we can more easily understand what our superior interests are, tuning ourselves in better to the energy currents with higher characteristics.

For this, it would be good to free ourselves from the negative emotional impacts of everyday life, attempting to relax in a disciplined way at particular hours and creating the healthy habit of reviewing through auto-analysis whether we are deviating from the evolutionary trajectory that we want for ourselves or are staying true to it. Contact with nature, taking a walk, or meditation exercise in a cozy spot can help. But it is also important to purify the physical body, through a balanced and healthy diet, freeing it from waste and toxins, along with making a habit of invigorating physical exercise.

An attitude of openness to life seems to make things easier, not being stuck to this or that scheme, to this or that situation, as remarkable or advantageous as it might have been; instead, cultivating a flexible, tolerant and available posture. In doing so, the person will be able to seize intuition more effectively, and therefore understand and react in an appropriate way, taking advantage of opportunities and letting life happen. And happen with pleasure, creativity, ease and a greater capacity for achievement.

◆ 18 ◆

Self-Healing and Healing

A RARE PHENOMENON FOR WHICH a plausible explanation is yet to be found is often called a miracle. But universal laws are natural and immutable and, as human knowledge advances, everything will be explainable.

Since ancient times, a belief has existed that physical and mental illnesses may have a corresponding spiritual weakness, because of a previous harmful act by the sufferer, or by action of one or more evil spirits. Currently, many spiritual people continue to believe in it, and many other people, although they claim not to believe, in moments of crisis resort to methods not proven by science to try to solve their problems. It has been scientifically demonstrated that human beings have the ability to interfere, by the action of thought, with the functioning of their own physical bodies and those of other living beings. However, within the current scientific paradigm, so-called spiritual healing, also known as spontaneous healing, is not properly explained yet.

There are various known healing methods; for example, intercessory prayer, therapeutic touch, Johrei, Qigong and Reiki (Benor 2007). In general, these healing methods are interpreted as a transmission of energy—of a nature not yet defined by science—with the intention of curing, from a therapist to a person. They are all somewhat scientifically studied, sometimes with positive and significant results (e.g., Baldwin et al. 2008; Hart, Freel et al. 2011; Wang et al. 2013), and other times without significant results (e.g., Assefi et al. 2008; Masters et al. 2006).

Intercessory prayer is the act of asking something of an entity considered superior, for oneself or for another person or other people (Dossey 1993). Commonly used in several religions, it may take diverse forms. It has been studied, sometimes with positive and significant results (e.g., Byrd 1988; Roe et al. 2015). It is believed that, in cases of successful healing, the good will of the therapist and his ability to connect with positive energy, channeling it to the patient, will join with the sincere desire of the patient to become pure, not only for the resolution of the situation for itself, but also for the correction, by his own effort, of the causes of the specific situation.

Therapeutic touch consists of the technique of the placing of hands on or above the patient with the express intent of rebalancing and harmonizing of the patient's energy system (Krieger 1975; Levin 2011). Its practitioners believe that the human body is part of a dynamic system of energy that interlinks physical, emotional, mental and spiritual aspects. Upon interfering with the magnetic field with the intention of healing, they aim to act on the different dimensions, thereby facilitating rebalancing. These therapists work in different stages. They begin by seeking to harmonize themselves and focus strongly on what they are about to do. They then concentrate on the sensitivity of their hands, in order to assess the situation through them. This is done by moving their hands at a distance of six to twelve centimeters from the patient's body. Having identified the imbalances or obstructions in the energetic field, via their own sensitivity, they move their hands to facilitate the flow of regenerative energy, until the balance in energy is restored.

Johrei is a healing and purifying method which is part of a life philosophy that appeared in Japan at the beginning of the 20th century, according to which what happens in the spiritual body is reflected in the physical body and vice versa. Within this philosophy, physical illness and psychological suffering appear as a result of negative thoughts, words and deeds, pollutants to body and spirit (Reece, Schwartz, Brooks and Nangle 2005). This healing method seeks to eliminate this pollution through the purification of the spiritual body, doing so via the flow of life energy channeled through the therapist's hands. Also in this case, it is important that the patient is willing to seek, through his own efforts, to do what is needed to remove the causes of the problem he is suffering, including possible behavioral errors.

Qigong is believed by its practitioners to be a way of manipulating (Gong) vital energy (Qi). Through deep states of relaxation and focus, they seek to optimize and balance the vital energy of the patient. Internal Qigong is a self-directed practice, where the practitioner seeks the flow and balance of vital energy in himself through relaxation, deep breathing and visualization techniques as well as meditation. External Qigong is a practice of interpersonal healing, in which the practitioner seeks to project life energy to another person to promote balance and health in that person (Ulbricht et al. 2010). Qigong, as well as being a therapeutic process, is considered a life philosophy, having as its principal objectives the tranquility and harmonization of the body and spirit with everything around them, from nature in general to people. This peace of spirit is managed in five phases: balancing of the body, of the breathing, of the mind, of life energy and of the spirit.

In Japanese, "Rei" means universal and "Ki" means life energy. "Reiki" means universal energy, with the meaning that everything in the universe is constituted of energy, which flows around and inside us. There is a field of energy intrinsic to all beings. Illness results from an imbalance in a center of energy, with repercussions on the physical body (De' Carli 2009; Miles and True 2003). The Reiki therapist seeks to channel life energy in such a way that the energy balance can be restored and, as a consequence, the illness cured. It is done by placing the hands in twelve different positions: on the head, on the front and back of the torso and sometimes in the areas affected by the illness. Patients mention a sensation of a vibrating flow of heat or cold, as well as a sensation of physical relaxation.

Mikao Usui, the founder of Reiki, instituted five principles for the interior development of practitioners: just for today, do not worry; just for today, do not anger; just for today honor your parents, teachers and elders; just for today earn your living honestly; just for today be grateful for all living beings. Reiki is, more and more, part of the range of services provided by hospitals in the world (Alarcão and Fonseca 2016; Ramos 2016). Reiki, and some other energy-based therapeutic practices, are also practiced at distance. In this case, the therapists seek to channel energy towards patients placed at distances, small or large, from them. The results of scientific studies of distant healing have not shown significant results, but they appear to suggest that expectations and belief in the results of the treatment are important factors in improving the clinical situation in some cases (Walach et al. 2008).

The principles described might explain these energy therapies and others, such as osteopathy, chiropractic, reflexology and even self-healing, but they do not explain surgeries carried out through mediumship when practitioners possess no theoretical knowledge of the surgery, and using only their hands and, in some cases, basic utensils such as knives and scissors. It is generally considered that further more rigorous and well-reported research is needed (Crawford et al. 2003; Radin, Schlitz and Baur 2015; Roe et al. 2015).

Many spiritual practitioners believe that spirits or souls liberated from the physical body might interfere in the life and health of human beings. This interference would tend to be favorable in the case of spirits with superior characteristics and unfavorable in the case of less-evolved spirits. This interference would only happen in conjunction with the kind of thoughts emitted by a person suffering the interference. If he thinks and acts constructively, he will create conditions for the favorable interference and avoid the harmful interference. If he thinks and acts negatively, favorable interference is less likely and harmful interference is favored.

In this framework, it might be admitted that a well-intentioned therapist could, by force of his positive thoughts, create conditions for the patient to liberate the negative charges which influenced him, making it possible for what seems to be a miracle to happen. This might be explained by the hypothesis that the therapist tunes into spiritual forces with massive energetic power, making him the medium through which they may be channeled. Apparently, this situation does not need any invocation of spirits or adoration rituals or supplication.

Relative to what is called spiritual healing, it must be considered that, if healing occurs through the influence of positive thought, he who is more spiritually evolved will be more effective in the practice. The conviction and desire of the therapist and the patient to resolve the situation also seem to have an important role. Finally, the ability in this activity must be considered, whether innate or acquired through training. However, it must be admitted that negative factors, such as vanity of the therapist or his commercial interests in the therapy, may prejudice success. In the case of the patient not seeking to eliminate the causes which triggered the problems, and not correcting his incorrect attitudes, relapse may naturally happen, until he puts his positive thoughts to work and corrects what he must correct.

It is realistic to accept that the universal laws cannot be distorted. If someone intends to reap some benefit, he must create conditions that promote it and win the right to enjoy it. It would counteract universal justice if, without any effort, an individual were to invoke the favors of any physical or spiritual entity and obtain that benefit. Anyone can be helped in the execution of an objective, including self-healing or healing, but that support appears according to the degree of success deserved, or rather, according to the merit of that individual.

Thus the importance of identifying the real causes of any problem or illness, as well as the correction or suppression of those causes, must be stressed—assuming as fundamental the role of good will, the wise use of free will and self-determination. In this way, independent of the techniques used, conditions may be created for rebalancing energy and, at the same time, tuning in to the energy of superior characteristics which may help in the resolution of problems.

But the use of strange, superstitious and commercial practices prejudiced enlightenment in these situations and discredited them. Despite this, scientific research might create better conditions for the better use of available energy, so that physicians and psychologists might better work with the human being, seen as a spiritual and physical whole. And for human beings to learn to better use all their potential, with responsible behavior in tune with universal laws.

◆ 19 ◆

Paradigm Shift

MODERN SCIENCE HAS MADE GREAT PROGRESS by using the methodology of repeatability, universality and objectivity. Scientists have developed their research with focused study on each part of the whole and, thus, discovered valuable knowledge for future generations. However, some phenomena at the edges have been ignored by science, certain interconnections between the parts and a wider perspective which embraces to a great extent the set of parts, or rather, the whole. More recently, some scientists in various countries and different universities have begun to open the path to enlightenment, through the research of all phenomena—even of parapsychological phenomena—assuming a more holistic view, trying to understand the totality that exists in each part and admitting the possibility that there exists a vast and invisible system of information to be studied with the greatest rigor.

Parapsychology is currently defined as a scientific discipline that studies the human and animal experience in which there appear to be interactions not currently explainable within the prevailing paradigms of time, space and known energies (Simões 2003). It uses the scientific method, although it studies phenomena which are generally spontaneous, sometimes unconscious, and as a result difficult to reproduce on demand in a research laboratory. While these phenomena have been statistically demonstrated, it is acknowledged that they might be better studied with an adaptation of the scientific method to be still developed.

Maybe because of the absence of widely accepted explanations for these phenomena within the scientific framework, maybe because some of them conflict with socially established ideas and prejudices, maybe because of opportunism, sensationalism and frauds perpetrated by unscrupulous people attempting to take advantage of human ignorance, parapsychology has been seen with suspicion and disbelief. However, over the 20th century, this scientific discipline gained the interest of a plethora of researchers from diverse fields: psychologists, physicians, nurses, physicists, mathematicians, etc. Parapsychological phenomena are currently studied in tens of universities, institutes and specialized laboratories, spread across the world, but mainly in Europe and North America.

Amongst the promoters of parapsychology stands out the North American psychologist Robert Morris, professor at Edinburgh University from 1985 to 2004, where he supervised 32 PhD students in parapsychology and became a respected researcher and lecturer. Morris made many visits to universities in Europe and the United States, where he promoted parapsychology and supported research being done in those institutions. His students and followers are, today, spread all over the world.

Parapsychological research has evolved, becoming extremely rigorous and demanding over the years. After a century of continuous work, many scientists are of the opinion that parapsychological phenomena produced under laboratory conditions are not sufficiently intense, nor sufficiently reproducible, for them to be officially accepted as natural facts, or robust enough to demand a change in the current scientific paradigm. However, impartial and objective analysis of spontaneous cases has encouraged acceptance of their existence among the general population, and continues to be a strong incentive for research to be sought and developed, until the area has been adequately explained. Add to that—as Stanley Krippner, professor of psychology and director of the Center of Consciousness Studies at Saybrook University, San Francisco, claims—parapsychological research is one of the sources of data that show us that our current view of the world is, in the best case, incomplete, and in the worst case, defective.

Bearing in mind the evidence, it is not reasonable for science to ignore parapsychological phenomena or claim that they do not exist. Science has the obligation to study them more and better, until there is a complete spiritual enlightenment of humanity. It falls to science to demystify some fantasies made up by shrewd exploiters of human ignorance; but it also falls to science to admit reality, whatever it may be, identifying all the potential energy in human beings, so that they may achieve better results while on this planet.

Many experiments conducted on telepathy and psychokinesis with humans and animals, following the rigor of the scientific method, are accepted scientifically. Will power is studied and respected; we can accept—by combining the results from research with knowledge in the area of spirituality—the importance of being able, through free will, to emit positive thoughts at every moment (reconnecting ourselves mentally to networks of positivity, facilitators of achieving good and useful things) or negative thoughts (reconnecting ourselves mentally to what is not good and creating conditions for things to go badly). People who see images that others do not see, those who hear sounds that others do not, and those who receive information about future occurrences which cannot be deduced from known data are considered normal people, and are studied and supported as such. Situations of psychiatric illness are, obviously, excluded. The phenomena of poltergeists and hauntings, while hard to study, have been more extensively researched by the academic world, leading towards their clarification and demystification. Scientific studies of near-death experiences, as well as supposed past lives, have naturally brought more acceptance of the possibility of the continuation of life after physical death. Surviving physical death has more recently been studied through instrumental transcommunication, which again argues for the necessity of more quality research, freed from the constraints of old taboos.

In this sense, a paradigm shift is now being proposed, while maintaining the rigor of the scientific method but becoming more comprehensive, pluralistic and holistic and accepting direct experiences. Alexander Moreira-Almeida (2013) argues that if we humbly recognize that our knowledge about consciousness is very limited and, at the same time, we audaciously, vigorously and creatively confront the mind-brain problem, as human beings we can march ahead towards a deeper understanding of our own nature. Hundreds of scientists from different disciplines subscribed to the "Manifesto for a Post-Materialist Science," published in 2014, which states, "Mind represents an aspect of reality as primordial as the physical world. Mind is fundamental in the universe, i.e., it cannot be derived from matter and reduced to anything more basic. [...] The shift from materialist science to post-materialist may be of vital importance to the evolution of the human civilization" (Beauregard et al. 2014, 273–274).

But for science to triumph in this area, it also seems necessary that researchers be in tune with universal laws. Research should be done with the greatest authenticity, without trying to reach this or that conclusion, but accepting the truth as truth. It should also be achieved with total detachment, without any economic or other interests, and with great simplicity, whatever the results, without thinking that they are fantastic. On the contrary, science should place itself at the service of humanity, with a great sense of usefulness. As one cannot have his cake and eat it too, researchers in the area of spiritual enlightenment, as well as volunteers with traits of mediumship, also cannot reconnect mentally to what is not good and, at the same time, obtain good results in their research. These good results will have a tendency to appear whenever the researchers and volunteers keep their thoughts positive and their attitude constructive, with pure intentions.

People in general—and also scientific researchers and mediums—will understand that the better way to feel fulfilled is by finding themselves, through contemplation and reflection—in subtler levels of consciousness, gaining another perspective of reality, distancing themselves from the many small problems in the day-to-day, tuning in to the superior interests of humanity, feeling at one with the universal whole, as a small particle. This contemplative attitude might provide the interior and exterior balance necessary for the definition of objectives that are more compatible with one's own superior interests and for inducing more suitable actions, allowing one to channel energy in a more appropriate way and, thus, obtain appreciable levels of efficacy. It becomes easier to abandon personal and selfish interests, focusing one's attention, thought and deed on what is, in fact, useful for others, for the whole and, therefore, also for oneself. It appears like an amplification of consciousness, permitting inner calm and silence, reinforced self-confidence and, then, the serene power of suitable actions, able to provide more beautiful achievements.

Lao Tzu, or Laozi, says, in the book *The Way*, "The sage manages affairs without action and spreads doctrines without words. All things arise, and he does not turn away from them. He produces them but does not take possession of them. He acts but does not rely on his own ability. He accomplishes his task but does not claim credit for it. It is precisely because he does not claim credit that his accomplishment remains with him" (Laozi and Chan 1963).

• 20 •

Transparency

TRUTH IS THE AGREEMENT OF THE IDEA with the object, the thought with the expression, the narrated fact with its reality. It is the quality by which things present themselves as they are. The use of the truth enables the human being to place himself within the natural laws, accepting himself with realism, as a particle of the universal whole. In that sense, it seems to be important that the habit of using it be cultivated from the crib, by parents giving their children healthy examples of truth in small day-to-day matters and in what are usually considered more complex questions, such as sex life and accepting one's errors, defining them as such.

To lie is to claim as true what is known to be false, or to deny what is known to be true, to cheat. To omit is to avoid saying or doing something, to not mention, to evade. To omit is to obscure the truth; it is, in a way, a form of lying. In this world of illusions and fantasies, appearances have been highly valued; however, they are chimeric, passing and, it goes without saying, secondary. From small to big things, we got used to living in lies as if they were the truth. But, at heart we know and feel that it is not true.

Even in the difficult cases of malignant diseases, it seems advantageous to use the whole truth, or better, the available truth, which permits the human being to have awareness of his state. Only consciously can he meditate on the causes of his disease and, duly supported psychological and physically, develop an appropriate reaction. Diverse cases of resolution of difficult clinical situations have been described, based on a patient's positive reaction, removing the causes of his pathology, opening himself to a healthier lifestyle, facing the future with optimism.

Transparency of attitude is, and will always be, highly valued. That which allows light to pass through and allows objects to be easily identified, seen clearly and evidently through it, is transparent. To be transparent is to be true, choosing to never omit, hide or lie. To be transparent is to let others know our thoughts as if they could see them.

Accepting that when we think we emit an invisible radiation which can be perceived by at least some people, we can theorize that we are all simultaneously senders and receivers of thought, although the capacity to receive differs from person to person (Jahn et al. 1997; May et al. 1990; Schmidt et al. 2004; Sheldrake 2004; Storm 2003; Radin 2006; Ullman and Krippner 1989). Some spiritualists further believe that spiritual beings who have freed themselves from their physical bodies have the ability to read our thoughts. They communicate with each other through thought and know everything we think, probably only having the capacity to understand in accordance with their evolutionary level.

According to this concept, we are transparent in our thoughts. If that is the case, that which is already evident to only a few sooner or later will become evident to all. It is worth reflecting a little on this perspective, and it would be useful for each of us, in our efforts to reach the truth, to accept this hypothesis. By accepting that when thinking we are emitting radiations that might be perceived by humans and any spiritual beings, we will conclude that lying is, after all, fooling only ourselves. Reality is what it is and others have ways of knowing it. But we have the ability to fantasize, acting as if it was possible to hide the truth, only wasting energy that could be put to better use. By accepting that our thoughts are or can be transparent to everyone around us, it will be easier to assume the simple, radiant, crystalline truth that can push us ever forward on the trajectory towards perfection that each of us is making.

The truth is what it is. It does not have to be imposed, nor should it be. It is to be accepted, with serenity, coherence, transparency. The truth is simple. Socrates said, "I only know that I know nothing."

The truth is courageous and persistent. Galileo, despite being condemned by the Holy Office of the Inquisition, maintained his theory that the Earth moved around the Sun: *"Eppur si muove* [however, it moves]." The truth is serene and tolerant. Jesus, unjustly condemned and crucified for seeking to enlighten humanity, professed: "Father, forgive them for they know not what they do."

As for the whole truth, it is still not available to the human being, the tiny inhabitant of such a small planet (when compared to the vastness of the universe). It seems that we get access to the truth as we employ honest investigative effort, in seeking enlightenment and ever more domain over universal knowledge. The whole truth must be unique and unified.

Sooner or later, all who announce it, along their various lines, will meet at the truth. The paths will become unified at The Path, not because it is obligatory but for the pleasure of being whole. Sooner or later, it seems everyone will be able to recognize universal values. Some—maybe too many—seem to remain distracted with other things. Others accept universal values, but act as though they don't recognize them. But, in the end, everyone will tend to feel them as their own, just they are everyone's, and will live with the progressive satisfaction of adopting them.

Perfection is an ideal, but it also seems to be practicable every day; if not in entirety, at least with a progressive approximation, and maybe even without regression. Perfection is consummation or completeness, sometimes material, but fully spiritual. It is something that corresponds to the full realization of all potential or virtues, which can and must be incentivized, supported, and cherished, but which it does not make sense to demand. The stairway to perfection is climbed step by step—and not by leaps and bounds—only when the self chooses to try to achieve it.

Jesus did not judge those who tortured him; he asked for forgiveness for them, because "they know not what they do." Gandhi was beaten several times without accusing his attackers because, he said, they were doing "what they thought right." Mandela left prison, where he had been imprisoned untried for more than quarter of a century, with an impressively serene look, with no vestige of hate. These positions of acceptance without judgment are sometimes difficult to understand or, thus, to follow.

Each thought, each word and each action is motivated by an intention and provokes an effect. Apparently, the universe doesn't judge. But a universal balance exists which involves everything and everyone, and which prefigures a full idea of justice. To become whole, the being must balance his energy, sometimes having the need to experience the effects that he caused.

Since we are responsible for our intentions, it is prudent and advisable for us to try to understand the effects such intentions provoke and seek to select them in accord with the effects we desire to produce. This involves the control of thoughts, words and deeds, even for the reciprocation of respective energy, in the ambit of the physical reality, for each action there is an equal and opposite reaction. People say, "Who sows the wind, reaps the whirlwind," a personalized way of understanding the balance of universal energy within the framework of an evolutionary journey which we all make in the world-school we inhabit.

For the interaction between beings to be fruitful, it is important to have a vision beyond immediate interests, with a universal perspective, which offers a lucidity of appreciation of those who are not yet perfect and still in an evolutionary phase. The feelings that appear will not be, then, of rage, rancor, revenge or depression, but naturally of comprehension, tolerance and compassion. As it is very difficult to understand the deepest reasons for each interaction and all the implications of those interactions, we must not judge what we see. It is healthy to identify negative situations, seeking to react positively in the materialization of our superior objectives, without getting involved in judging what does not concern us. It is not appropriate for us to allow for our reactions to be motivated by indignation, anger or victimization. These feelings result in poor judgment, in which we see ourselves as superior to those with whom we interact. Acting in this way, we do not develop the necessary strength to learn the life lesson in front of us, and we create further imbalances which, sooner or later, will turn against us.

Justice without judgment is a way of understanding everything in life, without involving negative emotions. It is the freedom to see what we see and try what we try, without negative reactions, or rather, without obstructing the healthy flow of intelligence, reason, solidarity and love. The Brazilian physician and university professor António Pinheiro Guedes (1983) believed most illnesses have their predisposing origins in the weakening of the spirit which, depressed and discouraged, does not communicate or transmit vitality to the body, vitality that is energy.

Happiness is expansive; it invigorates blood circulation, gives warmth and color to the body, animates and strengthens the organism, keeping it healthy, prolonging life.

Sadness, on the other hand, is focused inward; it slows the circulation, cools, takes color from the body, depresses and weakens the organism, damaging health, shortening life.

But, since extremes are reached and all that is in excess is bad, while depressing sadness makes existence dismal, happiness in excess is no less dangerous; it may even destroy.

The great truths can be told in a simple way. However, we curiously sometimes forget them and leave them out of our daily lives. We know that the more motivated we are to reach a determined objective, the easier it is to reach it. We also know that when problems appear, if we get discouraged, we distance ourselves from the path to success; if we stop believing or focus on defeat, it happens naturally.

We recognize that being a human who knows how to face reality with some optimism and a serene smile on his lips is on his way to triumph. Statistics show us that his life expectancy is greater. We know that the pessimist becomes whiny and that he who is whiny becomes pessimistic. Defeat is just a step away and illness just two or three. Psychosomatic illnesses are the proof of this, and many pathologies of the digestive, cardiovascular and respiratory systems, of the skin, etc., can be considered in this area, as well as depressions caused by various types of psychological problems.

We know all this but, here and there, we forget it. Or we think that it only happens to others. We know that the constant search for balance, for intelligent, rational and harmonious solutions, within a realistic and serene framework, with good humor, brings us a healthy life with relative material and spiritual success.

We also know that that is a valuable life and, as such, difficult to achieve. Difficult, but possible. Unequivocally possible if, and only if, we develop the necessary and adequate strengths by ourselves, re-motivating ourselves, animating ourselves, always with a positive perspective and a constructive attitude.

◆ 21 ◆

Discernment

DEVELOPMENT IN SCIENTIFIC RESEARCH in the area of parapsychology in the last few decades has been undertaken by researchers from many fields. Greater interest in the topic by academia can be seen, as can the possibility that in the 21st century much progress may be made, which will contribute decisively towards the spiritual enlightenment of humanity.

On accepting ourselves as a particle of energy temporarily inhabiting a physical body, we gain a more comprehensive and holistic perspective, coming to downplay mere physical phenomena and the materiality of things. We progressively understand the strength of our thoughts and how that influences our capacity for fulfillment. We come to assume responsibility for our words, for our attitudes and for all that happens to us. We understand that chance does not exist and that every attitude has its consequence; but, also, that all situations which we go through were caused by something within our responsibility.

We understand that the universe is ruled by natural and immutable laws which we progressively comprehend and accept, and to which we seek to tune in. Maybe initially because society pushes us in that direction, but then because our own consciousness obliges us to do so and, finally, because we find enormous pleasure in it. The pleasure of being ever more complete. The pleasure of being ever more equal to ourselves, in our best version. The pleasure of fusion with universal harmony; of fusion with universal intelligence; the pleasure of fusion with universal wisdom; of fusion with universal love.

We learn to accept others as they are, with their virtues and defects. We learn that it is not down to us to correct others; that is their responsibility. While they are not able to do so, they deserve our tolerance, with us understanding that, in their learning process on Earth, they still haven't learned to do better. And, whenever appropriate, they also deserve our constructive support, preferably without criticism or judgment on our part, without demands or impositions.

Desiring the world to be ever better, we end up understanding that the only thing which is down to us is improving ourselves, for which we need to develop an important strength. Focusing on ourselves, we can be useful to ourselves and, therefore, also to others, by giving them the example of our best selves. The spiritual perspective induces the awareness of an adequate management of the physical body. It is healthy to take part in good physical activity, enjoying the pleasures of the senses, but avoiding unhealthy exaggeration. It is good to remember that inappropriate behaviors tend to provoke pathological problems.

The acceptance of the law of cause and effect helps us understand the importance of prevention. It is always better to be safe than sorry. And, sooner or later, we understand the pleasure of balanced behavior. We understand the advantage of self-knowledge, the advantage of understanding ourselves and accepting how we really are, without looking to cheat others or ourselves. Understanding where we came from, where we are and where we should be going. Learning not to accuse ourselves for this or that. Accepting that we were already able to follow a certain path and we were still not able of going further. But with honest effort, we will be able to continue on our evolutionary trajectory successfully, which will provide us great satisfaction.

Using relaxation and meditation techniques, we get to know ourselves ever better, accepting ourselves as we are, accepting others as they are, perceiving ourselves as particles of the whole, progressively in fusion with it. Using reflection and by examining our conscience every day, we understand how to correct that which shames us, and we make progress through our efforts, perfecting ourselves, purifying ourselves. We learn to be at one with ourselves, with the others and with the whole. And, for us to know ourselves better, for us to meet ourselves, there is nothing better than a few minutes isolated from the world, in a quiet place, with the minimum noise possible, where we are not interrupted by other people, where it is neither hot nor cold and where we can be completely at ease. Placing ourselves in a comfortable position—for example, lying on our back or seated—in stillness, deeply relaxing, using one of the known techniques.

We can start by focusing our attention on the big toe of one foot, wishing it to be as relaxed as possible. When we feel it is, we extend this desire to the rest of the toes on that foot. Once achieved, we extend it to the whole foot, then the ankle, the calf, the knee and the thigh, until feeling that the whole leg is relaxed, soft, almost as if asleep. This exercise can be continued with the other leg, then one arm then the other. In the buttocks, the belly, the torso, the deep muscles of the spine, the neck, the face, the whole head, until we feel truly relaxed. Completely relaxed.

With practice, the relaxation exercise becomes easier and can be done in a few minutes. Meanwhile, we must divert our thinking away from the problems of the day-to-day lives, as if disconnecting from mundane worries. If, during the relaxation exercise, unwanted thoughts come to mind, they must be gently pushed away, while we focus our attention on the exercise itself. Only thus can we empty our minds of material worries, giving space to the meditation. There we will have conditions to better understand ourselves, including our spiritual dimension. It may not be on the first, second or third time, but with patience and serenity, the time will come for us when we find ourselves in a moment of expanded consciousness, which will happen with some emotion and much satisfaction.

Upon achieving a state of relaxation, it is advantageous for anyone to contemplate every day what they did the day before, how they would have liked to have acted and, in cases when they did not do so, what the determining factors were. When such factors are detected, it becomes easier to understand how to beat the situation, promising oneself to place all one's attention and energy in order that today the situation is not repeated. If we take stock daily, and promise ourselves honestly and firmly that we will not repeat that error that day, sooner or later, we will manage to not repeat it. On that day and on the day after and the day after that, until we understand—with much satisfaction—that we are free of that problem, that we have beaten it, that we have overcome it.

There are some people who like to accompany this type of exercise with prayers, previously organized mental radiations or other practices. They may not be necessary, but each person should find their own way, using whatever means seem most appropriate for themselves. And what seems appropriate for today might be different from what we thought appropriate some years ago.

Anyway, it is good for us to realize that the energy capable of making the most beautiful things is in us; universal energy, or divine energy, if you prefer, is in us. And the evolutionary trajectory we are taking is—and can only be—the fruit of our own efforts, our own worth. By doing the above exercise systematically, we develop the ability to stay attentive and focused on our day-to-day lives, tending automatically to assume realistic, positive, constructive attitudes. This will happen in a progressive way, in accord with our own force of will and our capacity for persistence.

Maintaining positive thought, assuming more correct attitudes—for us, for others, for the whole—in all situations, we create conditions for receiving the right intuition at the right moment, adding it to serene, constructive and superior reasoning. We become progressively more demanding of ourselves, but demanding in a balanced, healthy, luminous manner. We become progressively more tolerant of others, but with a constructive, supportive, friendly tolerance. We stop overvaluing the material delights of more primitive sensations.

We come to understand that happiness is in the achievement of good and useful things; that happiness is in the perfecting of ourselves; it is in our contributions to the achievements of others.

We learn to divert ourselves from what is no good, to control our thoughts, words and deeds, to have no fear of anything, to trust ourselves and, above all, in the universal laws. Progressively, nothing disturbs us, and we feel well.

This is progressive discernment. To discern is to understand what is real, understand what is more important, focus on what is lasting, to tune in to universal values. To discern is to know what is important to the whole, putting oneself constructively on one's path. To discern is to know: to know how to evolve and to know how to contribute towards evolution. To discern is almost to understand the universe, within the limits of an Earthly perspective, to feel like a particle, a wave of energy, with all its potential and possibilities to make that potential real, to tune in to the universe and its laws. All of this has nothing to do with social, economic or cultural status, or gender, race or religion.

Discernment is the consciousness of being part of the whole, accepting what is good for the whole, or for everyone, it is what prevails, to the detriment of the fulfillment of personal interests. Or, to put it another way, to make it so that superior and real personal fulfillment is integral to the fulfillment of the whole. And here is what is really important, what is useful, true, constructive, tolerant, good and beautiful. But to discern implies calm reflection about what is truly important, seeking the deepest part of oneself until one can hear one's voice as a particle of the whole, or rather, the voice of the whole heard through one's own voice. And then, determining how to stay focused on what is truly important, while following his evolutionary path.

Discernment also implies an effort of concentration, facing all the multiple social invitations, and one's own personal limiting tendencies, be they physical, psychic or mental. It implies implementing daily a system of taking control of situations, allowing an internal satisfaction of duties fulfilled, working in one's own favor and for others, tuning in to the real interests of the whole. Because of all of this, discernment is to learn, but also to accept. It is to understand but also to evolve. It is to know but also to love unconditionally.

The Science of Spirit

It is beautiful to understand who we are, but even more beautiful to analyze why we haven't been or how to become who we are. It is very beautiful to understand the potential we have in ourselves, but even more how to evolve and how we can support that evolution. It is extremely beautiful to feel that we know, but even more so to discover in ourselves the simplicity of what is integral or complete.

◆ 22 ◆

Discovering the Path

IN THE TIMES IN WHICH WE LIVE, it is important to stop. Knowing to stop to make a critical analysis of the path already trodden, contemplating failed opportunities and less useful options, as well as progress made thanks to developed strengths. It is a way of reviewing the path one has trodden, to know where one truly is and in what direction it will be best to head.

Analysis of a path, the path of each person, is a self-critical exercise. Not an exercise in apportioning responsibilities or seeking the guilty, but in admitting—from a spiritual perspective—that the one responsible for a person's path is that very person. Despite more or less strong influences, it seems that each person is the one truly responsible for that which happens to him.

It is important to analyze why, in the face of influence from third parties, we acted in a determined manner, whether it was the best way or not. To analyze what we should do in future similar circumstances to progress more favorably. How we prepare ourselves to do so with our resources, without physical or spiritual crutches, without waiting for a friend or family member to do what we are meant to do, or without resorting to asking a divine entity to help complete our tasks.

Thinking harmoniously, in tune with the universal whole, we create conditions for respecting universal laws and, thus, the laws of human beings. The fulfillment of being at one with our consciousness, the spiritual pleasure of feeling truly equal to ourselves—that which our deepest, intimate self-desires to be—far outweighs frivolous physical pleasures that we sometimes allow ourselves.

Concentrating on ourselves, we discover our own capacity for acting constructively in the face of the many situations of tension and small conflicts, of dilemmas and paradoxes, of our day-to-day lives. For acting without passivity but also without aggression, responsibly and serenely; with confidence, trusting more and more ourselves and nature. Then, we tend to act in harmony, conscious that positive efforts attract positivity. In the middle of complex situations, when there is no time to think about the various incorrect attitudes of others, we must be sufficiently mentally prepared and trained to carry on with determination, focused on our grand objectives.

At those times, the assertive attitude tends to use intuition, an enriching factor. One must understand that thought and action of a positive and constructive character create conditions to attract what is positive. It is necessary for one to think in a more elevated manner and act constructively, so that good intentions prevail. By acting constructively and accepting others and their differences, we create conditions to, sooner or later, develop the same attitudes in our surrounding environment. The positive attitude creates more favorable conditions for good accomplishments but also tends to have a contagious effect on others.

When everyone seeks to do their part, in an honest and focused way, they will discover their own path, and do it with a feeling of well-being which allows them to constantly renew their strength to continue their evolutionary trajectory with confidence and efficacy. Of course, there are moments in which we fail, but we can always correct ourselves, we can always make progress, we can always make our thoughts, words and deeds positive, as our deepest self— always—shows us.

We are in the world. We are part of the world. We do not always act according to our highest interests. We suffer from silly things, worry about trivial things and we even get to a point at which we have difficulty believing in ourselves. So it becomes important to stop. To know to stop, from time to time. To do a self-critical exercise to analyze our own path. When we ask ourselves why we went wrong, when we question ourselves about wandering without direction, we end up by finding the direction, by correcting the error and discovering the more suitable path.

It seems right to do a balancing of accounts of our lives two or three times a year, contemplating our major life goals and how to achieve them. Seeking, also, to know ourselves better, identifying our own strengths and weaknesses and trying to define how to correct the latter, helping to keep us on our evolutionary trajectory. And then, we get used to saving ten or fifteen minutes per day to relax and seek our true self, using whatever means each person finds most convenient, from meditation to reflection.

When we stop, disconnecting ourselves from the turbulence of the world, we always have our own interior serenity available to us, and the more we disconnect, the more serenity we feel. And the more serenity we feel, the more lucid we become, downplaying day-to-day occurrences and positively constructing our thoughts. By increasing lucidity, we are in better condition to assess situations. The analysis of what we did the day before that shamed us, seeking the reasons for that behavior and looking for solutions, promising ourselves not to repeat that attitude the next day, might be called a daily examination of our conscience, and it is of great use in our spiritual progress.

When it is done with pure intentions, abstracting oneself from the world for a few minutes, this conscience examination can be highly effective, whether for mental hygiene, or as a means towards correcting our errors. The daily self-promise to not repeat the error of that other day might be made over and over, during weeks, months or years but, as already mentioned, the honest practice of analyzing one's conscience allows us one day to realize that we do not tend to make that error any more, that it is already a part of our past, that we overcame it. And those are moments of great joy, for having done something which we understand as an eternal value, won forever.

All of us, or almost all, worry about our daily physical hygiene, but in a time in which the surrounding world is often detrimental, sometimes aggressively so and, almost without us noticing, contaminating, it seems to be more and more important to maintain strong and heightened thoughts, so it is good for us to also worry about our daily mental hygiene. Mental hygiene seems to be more easily achieved in connection with nature; in the development of a physically and intellectually intense activity, while not exaggerated to avoid stress; in the practice of a sport; by participating in charitable or cultural activities. It is good to avoid noisy environments or other kinds of pollution; worshipping excess, like consumerism; and places of vice, whatever they might be. Maybe also the places of mystical practices. It seems important not to pay too much attention to, nor fill our conversations with, calamities, violence, illness, hatred, vanity or eroticism.

Then, in our day to day, we should seek to develop simple, clear and pure ideas, making our behavior coherent and transparent, in the defense of universal values, without wavering, by harmoniously accepting the just, the good and the beautiful. Respecting everything and everyone, it is natural for us to admire exemplary behavior and to seek to be with those who can offer us good teaching, independent of their social, economic or intellectual levels. It is advisable to maintain these kinds of decisions when reading the newspaper, watching television, navigating the internet or choosing a film to watch.

Keeping positive thoughts twenty-four hours a day means sleeping well, which can be aided by calm and constructive reading before going to bed. A good sleep provides us a recovery of our energy, which allows us to better follow our own path, resisting external pressures that always appear in our way. If daily physical hygiene keeps us relatively unscathed from attacks by bacteria, viruses and other pathogens, mental hygiene seems to also create some kind of invisible shield, defending us from outside aggressions, strengthening our capacity to accomplish our higher interests. By hygienically making our thoughts positive, we seem to naturally repel what is negative, making us a focus of transmission and attraction of positivity.

The meditation exercise, when well done, allows us to reach a higher state of consciousness—different from wakefulness, dreaming and sleep—which enables great lucidity, in growing symphony with the universal harmony. And this expanded state of consciousness, which begins by being temporary, tends to become permanent in our day-to-day life with practice, and with constant perfecting of the individual. Many people look everywhere for solutions to their problems, and for someone who will help them to find their path, while all along the solutions are within them. While it is the understanding of their own nature that allows them to find the meaning of their actions on this planet. While, after all, it is up to them, and only them, to define their own path.

• 23 •

Universal Values

Correct words are not always pleasant.
Pleasant words are not always correct.
Good men never argue.
Those who argue are not good.
Wise men are not necessarily educated.
Educated men are not necessarily wise.
Wise men own nothing, keep nothing in their memory,
    but serve all and in this, they possess everything.
In the end, they conquer what they never desired, since they
    continuously give themselves to everyone.

THIS IS A BEAUTIFUL PASSAGE FROM the philosopher Lao Tzu in the book *The Way of Lao Tzu*. It is worth rereading and meditating on it a little.

After all, simplicity, serene and courageous defense of the truth, without conflict, without confusion, are universal values. Mankind is discovering that universal wisdom does not limit itself to technological knowledge and is far beyond the conquest of material wealth. He continues to discover that those who ask nothing for themselves and wish nothing for themselves achieve everything, even if they do not desire it.

These are the truly wise. They who create conditions for themselves to never been stepped on by others, but who also never stand over others. Who never seek tasks or responsibility for which they do not feel ready, but who try to fully accomplish that with which they have been entrusted; who always feel equal to others, whether with intellectuals or the illiterate. Who tolerate false demonstrations of wisdom in the ignorant, remaining calmly available to help them find the true knowledge; who consider themselves always as apprentices.

When each of us decides to be authentic in our posture, to try to align with universal values with genuine transparency, as much as our current evolutionary level allows, and wanting to progress according to all our potential, then each of us is authentic. It is not necessary to worry about helping others or accomplishing this or that mission because, being what we are, we are already helping and opportunities to be useful will appear naturally. When someone looks for someone else to help, that person is probably not the right person to be helping; he may just be interfering with the lives of others. It is already a very good thing not to undermine others with our attitudes. It is even better if we offer them the example of balanced behavior, with a healthy mind. It is better to wait for people to come to us, looking for our help, even if not asking explicitly. At that time, they show trust in us and are open to expressing their experience. Then our support flows freely.

But remember that helping someone is not giving them or imposing a solution upon them. Helping someone is presenting new perspectives about the problem that troubles them; it is opening a window to a different path, and then letting the person ponder and decide what is the best path for them. Only thus will the other person be making their own evolution. Only thus will we be truly useful.

Sometimes the man who loves his wife would like to possess her so deeply that it is as if he were nourishing himself from her. Sometimes the woman who loves her husband would like him to be an exact copy of her ideal man. Sometimes, parents want to mold their children according to their own ideas. Sometimes, some people try to convince their friends whom they want to help that their own perspectives are the ones which would be most appropriate to the friends' problems.

But these possessive ways of loving are too limiting to be truly fruitful. True love, spiritual love, seems to be authenticity, freedom, and respect for those close by. True love seems to give without demanding, without asking, without expecting anything in return. Spiritual love seems to be just giving oneself.

Those who wish to help others in the possessive way become permanently dissatisfied, because they can never reach their unrealistic and unnatural goals. Those who maintain a giving posture will feel happy, some more than others. Happiness may be felt less in those who try to give what is theirs, what they have, and certainly more in those who are aware that they have nothing to give, because, after all, they own nothing, apart from experiences lived and their ability to tune in to universal wisdom, which they share with deep pleasure.

It seems to be undeniable that there are constant values which exist beyond the material, which we understand as ideal ones and to which we want to adhere, although, sometimes—or even often—we have difficulty in doing so. We consider them universal probably because they are valid for everything and everyone and because they prevail above all else. The embracing of such values comes from a journey of individual learning, through calm analysis, from a constant search for constructive, intelligent and rational solutions, beneficial to everything and everyone. In the school of life there are always opportunities for learning, seeking to correct our bad habits and overcoming our imperfections.

On seeking to tune in to universal values, on making ourselves open to learning, on assuming our own responsibility and seeking to do our part, each human being creates conditions for harmonizing with the energy that is always available. And, thus, things happen, beautiful things. In this way, we make spiritual progress. And when we are truly tuned in to universal values, we feel an enormous sense of inner fulfillment, which is sometimes hard to describe but which can take sublime shape, making us vibrate until there are tears in our eyes.

We all know the importance of values such as integrity, which is not limited to paying the right amount or fulfilling a commitment on time. It also extends to loyalty in how we behave, and rectitude in fulfilling our duties, such as dedication to our work, which enables us to do good, benefiting the other and helping progress in general. It extends to the value of assuming truth as truth, whatever happens, with thought, moderation and in the spirit of justice. It extends to being demanding, above all with oneself, but tolerant with others and always constructively supportive, respecting everything and everyone. To have courage to face problems and to serenely defend the position that one believes to be the most useful, with detachment, simplicity, self-control and good sense, in a balanced and honest way, even when the majority, and/or those who have material power, defend another position.

It seems that by assuming universal values, the individual becomes aware that he is no more nor less than the others. He sees himself as a particle of energy and learns to use this perspective increasingly for the benefit of others, permitting further effectiveness and an increase in his own sense of fulfillment. With improvement, his personality gains the spirit of conquest and seeks to further develop his own characteristics. Perhaps his evolutionary trajectory will culminate in his fusing with the energy that animates the universe, meaning the evolution of personality until it is depersonalized.

Personality is the way of being, acting, reacting that characterizes the individual and distinguishes him from others, subjectively appearing as the emergence of the self from reflexive consciousness. Maybe becoming stronger the closer it gets to others, rooting itself progressively into a collective or universal consciousness.

Character is the conjunction of universal values which an individual has permanently accepted as his own, which can be witnessed in his behavior. It acts as a mark or an imprint which morally distinguishes him from any other person. There are those who consider it as "the mental skeleton of a person," implying his notion of reality, permanence, solidity and, sometimes, invariability. Reality because it is what it is, apart from illusory fantasies; permanence because it deals with something acquired, which then remains permanently; solidity for being like a psychic structure upon which the adaptation of the individual to the environment is taking place; invariability for his evolutionary process being slow and gradual, apparently static in the short term.

Character reveals itself through the honesty of one's conduct and one's degree of resistance to unworthy attitudes, like dishonesty, envy, slander, intrigue, disloyalty and deceitfulness in general. It expresses the spiritual level of the person, being assessed by the firmness and rectitude of his daily actions. As an individual way of adapting to one's surroundings, character is the conjunction of characteristics of someone, the sum of one's own congenital dispositions, and their modification by the influence of the environment, and by one's own effort and action.

Factors from psychic inheritance, linked to biological elements, add—from a spiritual perspective—to the lessons learned by the individual in possible previous physical lives. Then the education or shaping of character has a part to play, orienting, correcting and developing congenital dispositions, where parents, teachers and educators in general have an important role. In the formation of character, it is important to provide elements which allow the organization of an educational ideal, for which the cultural level, without being essential, is a facilitating factor. But the strength of the example that these educators may offer will tend to exert a fundamental influence on the pupils. The influence of public figures of the past and present, although more remote, should not be underestimated.

Finally, there is the difficult individual work of refining the character. Here, it seems to be important that the subject knows himself, with a realistic and balanced perspective; that he seeks to perfect himself, setting clear and concrete objectives; and that he carefully selects suitable means to achieve such objectives, taking into account his personal reality, aspirations and outlined objectives. All this demands long periods of meditation and self-analysis, performed periodically, in which it is advisable to carry out a daily exercise of self-control and assessment, driven by a strong and persistent desire toward natural perfection.

The injustices, ingratitude, deceit and grievances which a person may suffer can make it easier for him to perceive human depravity, causing him anger and then disgust. This disgust will cause the ever clearer and deeper conviction for the need to be free of negative conduct, after which will follow the pleasure of the positive attitude and constructive action, in growing harmony with universal values. This harmonization with universal values seems to be slow, progressive and with no turning back. There is no place for great evolutionary leaps, fruit of luck or miracles. Everyone, by himself, does justice to his own evolution, by refining his character. Nor will there be any turns back; that is, accomplishments made will be definitive, true spiritual richness accumulated over time.

As each individual learns to tune in to universal values, he must come to know exactly how to occupy "his" space in the whole, respecting the other particles of the whole with tolerance. Then, he will feel universal wisdom reflected in him in all its splendor. Citing Lao Tzu again:

> The incomplete will be completed.
> The empty, filled.
> The spent, renewed.
> The insufficient, increased.
> The excessive, dissipated.
> This is why wise men embrace Unity
> seeing it as a model of the Universe.
> As they never stand out, they shine.
> As they are never vainglorious, they have merit.
> Because they never fight, nobody opposes them.
> The Ancients said:
> That which is incomplete will be completed.
> Is that a phrase in vain?
> In the end, everything will be returned to perfect integrity.

• 24 •

Responsibility

THE UNIVERSE IS RULED BY NATURAL and apparently immutable laws. Ruled by the law of cause and effect, each and every thought, word or attitude will cause a particular effect. Each and every situation has a particular cause as its origin. It should be emphasized also that a thought generates a certain effect; and behind an attitude there is always a generating thought.

This concept is beautiful, because it makes something or someone responsible. In fact, according to this law, we are always responsible for what happens to us. Our present is a result of our past. If we know how to be constructive, positive, diligent, correct, we conquer the right to live in relative happiness. If, on the other hand, we are careless, lazy, negative, destructive, malicious, we suffer the consequences of the bad use of our free will. Of course, the family, social or work environment where we find ourselves have an influence on how our life unfolds. But, responsibly, our presence in these environments owes itself to our choices, it being always possible to influence and be influenced, but in this case we consent to it.

There are those who limit this concept to the present physical life and others who consider it to be eternal. The former look for causes of their current suffering in their bad behavior since childhood. The latter accept that they may be suffering due to incorrect attitudes in supposed previous lives. Both claim that the harm we do to others will come back to bite us—in a boomerang effect—and that the good we do will come back to us as good. Thus, in the present, we are constructing our future, which will be that much better, the more we try to tune in to the said universal laws.

With this idea, chance does not exist. Everything has a reason to be, although it is sometimes very difficult to discover the remote causes of the situations we are living at this moment. It is, however, necessary to be careful not to exaggerate this way of thinking, which is frequently done, regarding destiny—in a fatalistic sense—by people who feel condemned to certain situations, feeling that it is not worth trying to alter the direction of their lives.

But it is not so. The individual who commits a horrific crime needs to learn that it is wrong, to repent and to correct himself, creating conditions so that he never repeats the crime. In the moment that he effectively corrects that part of his own self, he frees himself from the negative situation he was buried in, without needing to suffer more in himself the horrors of crime that he perpetrated. Only in the case of not being aware of the harm he has done and not correcting himself will suffering of that kind, or similar, fall upon him again, as many times as necessary until he wakes up to the reality of his incorrect behavior and understands that the only way of freeing himself is to not stain his spiritual résumé further with similar attitudes. Rather, he must seek to enrich this résumé with actions of an opposite signal, of generosity, giving, dedication to others, love of others. When he does so, he will no longer need to be punished nor forgiven. It would not make sense. It seems far more logical that everyone wins his right, through his own effort, to free himself from his errors and reach a state of greater spiritual evolution, which will provide him relative happiness.

Those who meditate deeply on the law of cause and effect seem to create conditions for finding their path of balance and harmony with the universal laws, for giving up blaming others for failures, for ceasing to be afraid of the bad luck that follows them. For stopping lamenting the suffering they have been through, for giving up fearing not being able to beat the difficulties in their lives, for stopping asking or begging others for the resolution to their problems.

Those who meditate deeply on the law of cause and effect become more responsible, more confident in themselves, more convinced of their own abilities, more decisive in keeping their thoughts positive and in developing the strength necessary to conquer their right to resolve their errors, difficulties and problems. The human being who strives for enlightenment must come to understand that he has sufficient power to change the course of life, understanding that the future that he projects for himself is being constructed now. Then he lives in the present with his eyes on the future; since those who do good, do good to themselves, and those who do wrong, do wrong to themselves.

Particular attitudes that the individual assumes will cause respective effects. But it should be noted that this attitude is already a result of a particular thought, which originated it. Then, on controlling his thoughts, the individual controls his attitudes and, thus, shapes his future, naturally in accord with his current level of evolution.

Accepting that human beings are on the Earth to undertake a path of learning, which translates as self-improvement, it would be good to consider the level of responsibility that each has in his own evolutionary trajectory. In difficult moments of that trajectory, it becomes necessary to be prudent and patient, maintaining a strong link to universal values, in the search for solutions—by inner renewal and restructuring—which lead to constructive attitudes, while preserving tranquility of conscience. Thus the energy of superior characteristics flows with greater intensity. Thus is built a better world, from the inside outwards.

In these difficult moments, though, many people seek solutions that come from the outside inwards, or rather, they wait for others to solve their problems. They ask for the collaboration of families or friends. They ask or beg for the support of spiritual beings. It is understood that the others can help—in the physical and/or astral plane—but that the self is the being truly responsible for one's own trajectory. It falls to each person to build his own path. While he does not do this, it remains to be built. But when he accepts that he should do it, he discovers, through his own inner renewal, the enormous potential at his disposal to realize that path. In the resolution of problems, the person feels great inner fulfillment and creates the incentive to continue and seek in himself an increase in ability for the resolution of ever greater problems. Upon discovering and fulfilling his own potential, the individual proceeds as if finding himself, enjoying the true pleasure of being.

When attention and energy reconnect to what is higher and elevating, they create conditions for the resolution of problems, but it can also be accepted that they create spiritual conditions for the intervention of beings of superior characteristics, at the same time impeding malevolent actions by less evolved beings. But the human is truly the one responsible for everything that happens to him. The idea of it being an obligation to answer for one's own actions, or—under certain circumstances—for actions of others, or for something trusted to him, seems to be something fundamental in life.

When one is in a position of responsibility, besides the obligation to be responsible, the question is to whom are you responsible? To what entity was the commitment made? The full meaning of the term *responsible* seems to imply the existence of someone to whom the individual feels permanently bound: the creating entity of all things, the universal whole. Considering the human being as a particle of that whole, being aware of this, maybe it can be accepted that the individual is responsible, in the first place, to himself, or to his conscience as a representative of the universal consciousness.

In a similar way to what happens with most of the characteristics of beings, responsibility seems to have various levels and assumes a progressive shape; with successful experiences we become more responsible. In which case, it is good to focus our attention on beneficial exercises in the development of responsibility.

After a few years of practicing a martial art, for example, an individual might be embarrassed to say that a colleague succeeded in hitting him during training. Since he was trained for a long time to avoid or defend himself from attack, by using the available energy, the practitioner feels a progressive responsibility which leads him to believe and claim, "I consented to be hit." In fact, when someone hits someone else, there is a division of responsibility. The intention of aggression is the responsibility of the aggressor and the action of the aggression is the responsibility of the aggressor. But, faced with the intent and the act, the absence of defense which permits the impact is the responsibility of the victim.

Martial arts can and should allow a growing sense of responsibility in the practitioner in all his actions, from the development of constant attention to everything which goes on around him, to the assumption of a pragmatic realism which makes him avoid situations of possible conflict, seeking to use the available energy in the most useful way possible. In the school of life, does not the same thing happen? Are we not, over time, persistently subjected to many aggressions, not just physical, which allow us to learn to avoid situations or to defend ourselves from all kinds of attack, using the energy available to us at that moment?

In any situation of aggression, the responsibility of intent belongs to the aggressor; the act of aggression, also. But, faced with the intent and the formation of the action, it seems to be our obligation to realize the situation and avoid it or defend ourselves. Our responsibility is in the option of using, or not, the available energy, and in the option of using that energy only to defend ourselves or to also use it to counterattack.

In our day-to-day lives, more than in martial arts, it seems evident that the use of available energy should be in the positive sense, constructively, so that the counterattack will be assimilated as an educational act of non-aggression and a conquering of peace. In other words, the master of martial arts is not he who after an effective defense applies a mortal counterattack, but he who, as an exemplar, uses the available energy to teach effective, pragmatic, confident, serene and pacifying defense. In real life, to love is not to be conniving with the malevolence of those who intend to harm or injure us, nor peacefully consent to our damage when attacked. To love is to maintain serenity and seek to always think constructively, wanting to find the best solution for oneself, for the other and for all.

The best for the victim of aggression is to avoid the aggression, maintaining one's route serenely and firmly. But it is also important to be respected, distancing oneself, making the aggressor understand that his aggressive attitude was wrong and that it would be advantageous to correct that attitude. To turn the other cheek is to show respect, which is always due the victim and the aggressor. To turn the other cheek is not a gesture of counterattack, of animosity, rancor or hate. That would be a lack of respect towards the other and towards oneself. The fact that the aggressor is acting with ill-intent does not give the victim the right to respond aggressively or negatively. In this way, the two of them would be acting in an incorrect manner.

A considerable number of human beings sometimes say awful things, including to the people closest to them, which they later regret and feel ashamed about, but they do not have the courage to assume responsibility and apologize. When someone learns to control his thoughts, he can distinguish his own thoughts from those he captures from outside, controlling himself and seeking to maintain positive thoughts, so that intuitions which come to him may also be positive. He assumes responsibility for the bad things he says, apologizes and progressively controls his words.

When he learns to control what he says he also learns to control what he does, becoming increasingly constructive and effective in his acts, assuming responsibility for his acts until he learns how to internalize that everything that happens to him is his responsibility. It might be asked what responsibility the airplane passenger bears if it crashes, with the death of all its occupants. But the truth is that, in these cases, there always appear to be passengers who were going to fly on that plane but who, for one reason or another, decided not to. Those who decided to board the flight did so of their own will. Those who had the intuition not to, did not board of their own will, of their own responsibility.

In real life, one might call master he who takes full responsibility for his thoughts, words and actions, and also everything that happens to him, serenely paying constant attention to everything that happens in and around him, assuming a pragmatic realism which makes him divert situations of possible conflict, seeking to use the available energy in the most useful way for him and for the whole. Thus he also creates conditions for himself to benefit from suitable intuition at the right moment which, after all, is also his responsibility.

In the individual future, it seems realistic and advantageous that each person—although subject to environmental circumstances—is the one responsible for what happens to him. If the human being really wants to prepare his future adequately, he makes conditions to do so, without forgetting that evolution is progressive, that he cannot jump ahead. Just as a student in 3rd grade cannot suddenly leap to 10th grade, spiritually, it is necessary to develop the strength necessary to progress in a consistent manner and as fast as possible.

As for the collective future, we all know that humanity is, more and more, living an anti-nature lifestyle. We destroy twenty hectares of forest per minute, which means eleven million hectares per year. In any kitchen today, we have more chemical products than a chemist's laboratory would have had a hundred years ago. Every minute, two hundred tons of highly toxic product are produced. We throw seven million tons of trash into the sea every year. We must admit and accept that by taking the Earth away from its natural point of balance, there will be a logical natural reaction (by nature herself), which will probably be as drastic as humankind's attitudes are out of balance.

However, some philosophers—among them Agostinho da Silva—think that the human being of the 21st century will return more to his spiritual life, rejecting the frenetic material race in which we lived in the 20th century. Respecting the universal laws, seeking intelligent solutions, living in a rational way, constructing sustainable organizations, investing in scientific research, we will logically be building a better future for humanity, on the way to rebalancing attitudes and spiritual enlightenment.

• 25 •

Learning to Think

I T IS OFTEN IN MOMENTS OF GREAT PHYSICAL or psychic suffering that man analyzes his own attitudes, his way of thinking and acting, and admits that he has contributed to the situation which ails him. He seeks, then, to detect the causes of the suffering and what he should correct to improve and resolve the situation in the present and for the future. This is how he perfects himself; this is how he discovers new opportunities for development; this is how he can propel himself and even others to complete sometimes incredible tasks. Very often suffering serves, after all, for us to discover the way to perfection and success!

And for the collective, doesn't something similar happen, too? Do families not discover, in moments of suffering, conditions for achieving beautiful things for their members and for the collective? Shouldn't all diverse institutions, when in troubling situations, seek to correct the attitudes that contributed to those situations, trying to design a more successful trajectory and make the effort towards accomplishing it?

And does the same not apply to countries? When the collective condition is not comfortable, should not governments and the governed seek to correct what brought them to this point, trying to find suitable solutions for a good present and a better future? And for humanity in general would it not also be desirable, when in a general crisis, to seek to serenely and honestly detect the causes, plan to correct and resolve them constructively, for the benefit of all?

Above all, in moments of confusion, it seems of the greatest importance that each person knows how to concentrate on the essential, creating conditions to do his part and not let himself become embroiled in disturbing situations. Even if others don't fulfill their obligations, even if others take nonsensical actions, it is crucial that each is able to understand the importance of focusing on fulfilling his duty and of making things happen in the most useful way possible. Our best contribution is to do our part, independently of what is going on around us. And if this is important and valuable in normal situations, it is even more so in situations of greater crisis, for the deed in itself and for the example that it demonstrates, positively influencing third parties.

To do our part, it is important to begin by knowing how to position our thoughts, contemplating what can and should be learned, taking into consideration that the human capacity for learning seems to be enormous, constant, with hard to define limits, a source of great inner pleasure, sometimes of surprising dimensions. It is interesting the way in which it is possible to cultivate a certain kind of thought, shaping what will happen next. To learn to select these thoughts amidst everything else that comes to our minds, perfecting a way to keep them and, at the same time, reject the others, learning to concentrate our attention on what is important.

And it is interesting how a strong, clear and well-aimed thought driven by conscious will power seems to create better conditions for achieving an ideal, from the small questions of our day-to-day lives to our major objectives. We don't always value the importance of learning to focus on a specific subject, of seeking to gather and interconnect all the information, and of letting our imagination wander, trying to discover all of its characteristics, all of its interpretations, all of its implications. It becomes very pleasant, however, to understand how this exercise is profoundly enriching in the opening up perspectives and in preparing suitable conditions for us to realize our goals.

On making this journey, we understand how important it is to analyze a situation impartially, avoiding influence by prejudice, taboos, sympathies, self-interest or even by the presumption that we already know or dominate this or that. Finally, we understand the importance of the essential part of subjects, that is, of how they can be truly useful for the self, for those around us and for the whole. It may even be surprising how a limpid, constructive, crystalline thought seems to make itself a pole that attracts energy with the same positive signal, becoming a powerful tool. Apparently, a strong thought with positive characteristics attracts positive energy, creating conditions for overriding what is not important and even repelling what is destructive, negative and of inferior characteristics. It also seems clear that when an individual allows himself to become entangled in disconnected thoughts, he becomes entangled in his own web. Or when he allows himself to be taken by destructive, selfish, perverse or evil thoughts, he seems to attract energy with the same signal, becoming a pole of negativity, until he resolves to invert the situation, by influence of his own will placed at the service of his greater interests.

The vitality of thought in a well-intentioned individual, one who seeks enlightenment and to be useful to himself and to others, seems to grow through strong will and even according to his necessities, amplified and expanded in a way that overcomes the difficulties that appear. And learning from this reality brings growing inner fulfillment, just as the capacity for subsequent realization brings useful results for him and, above all, for others (Besant and Leadbeater 1901). But, sometimes, malevolent, disturbing situations appear to us which seem to be hard to solve. It is worth considering how to fight or beat them. In his book *The Seat of the Soul,* Gary Zukav (2014) claims, "An army can engage another army, but it cannot engage evil. A compassionate heart can engage evil directly—it can bring Light where there was no Light" (56). Evil can be understood as the absence of light, a lack of enlightenment. Being an absence, it needs to be filled—not exactly combated, but filled. Never fought by evil, but filled with enlightenment, with light. Hate fought with hate cannot diminish, only increase.

To fight evil, considering the absence of light, implies looking with firmness, but also with tolerance and compassion, at those who practice it, trying to understand its causes and seeking to create conditions for their removal or correction. And these conditions may be the most diverse, from cultural to economic, from environmental to spiritual. When hate provokes aggression, the best way for the victim to contribute towards the elimination of evil may be to seek to understand what in himself provoked the aggression and to correct what there is to correct. Thus, he can contribute decisively towards the filling, the enlightenment, of the malevolent situation.

This is not to say that we must ignore bad attitudes or behaviors, towards which we must use firmness. Rather, a solution should be sought, with intelligence and, above all, with love, that goes to the root of the question and that has the courage and strength to bring effective enlightenment to all parties. Even if others do not do so, even if the majority do not, it seems genuinely important for each human being to find in himself sufficient energy to think and act positively. By himself and for himself, for others, and for the whole. Not for doing what falls to the others to do, but to do what falls to him to do, in favor of the whole.

Every one of us seems to be a small particle of universal energy (Dossey 2013, 2014), reflecting in itself the potential of the whole and remaining interconnected to all the other particles of the same whole (Eckartshausen 2003). However, many people seem to behave as if their lives are completely separate from the others, defending their own interests in a selfish manner, paying little attention to the interests of their families, friends and colleagues, without showing any consideration or interest for the others. But consciousness of being a particle of the whole induces a more altruistic, supportive way of thinking and brings a growing automation in behaviors of the same kind, even to the clear privilege of the interests of the whole. It seems possible and desirable to be supportive even of the ill-doers; not of their objectionable attitudes, which always deserve firmness, but of what they need for their recovery.

This sense of solidarity embraces the animal kingdom—dogs or cock fights will end when the vast majority of people believe them to be criminal—and the plant kingdom—soulless deforestation and man-made fires will end when the majority finally respects nature.

This solidarity will go from mere thought to action, until it becomes a permanent state of spirit. On learning to think, the human being identifies himself as a particle of the universal whole, progressively understanding how it is reflected in himself; but also understanding his natural projection and integration in the whole. On understanding himself in the totality, the ego diminishes, and the true self reveals itself, in fusion with the whole.

• 26 •

Whole Truth

THE TRUTH IS IN THE TORAH, in the five books of Moses; in Lao Tzu's Book of the Perfect Path; in Confucius's Anthology. It is also in the Hindu Bhagavad Gita and Buddha's Dhammapada. The truth is in the Christian Bible, in the Muslim Koran, in the Tibetan Book of the Dead and in many other books.

Some very evolved spiritual beings that passed time on Earth demonstrated exemplary conduct and left wonderful messages of spiritual enlightenment and behavioral orientation. These messages arrive to us through books written by those beings or, for the majority of such books, admirers who took the responsibility, with their limitations, of transcribing them. In all these books we find important contributions to the enlightenment of humanity. In all of them we seem to find parcels of truth, although in none of them the whole truth, but we get the feeling that there exists an essential axis common to all, or almost all, of them.

There are complementary aspects added, often presented, and maybe even formatted, by the followers, where the differences are intensified, but there remains a feeling that, in essence, the messages from the grand masters are very similar. All of them will have sought to show the path to enlightenment, to show how everyone has at his disposal everything he needs to progress, accessing increasing parcels of truth. And this happens in accordance with our efforts to learn, in perfecting ourselves, in our progress; in accordance with our merit.

It would be reasonable to accept that this learning can be done with any of the books which are considered sacred, maybe more so the less sacred we consider them. Maybe even more when, with freedom, the different books are studied and the respective lines of thought analyzed. Certainly even more so when we know better how to put into practice the lessons learned, enriching our experience of life.

Keeping the essence of the messages from the masters, the concepts, the doctrines, the religions themselves seem to evolve, expunging the unnecessary, unimportant and even inconvenient. The global movement that results from that is the confluence of nearing the whole truth, unique and unifying. But apart from the big religious leaders, it is not difficult to find beings around us, much simpler and more discreet, who seem to live in the purity of important parcels of truth. They are, for now, a minority, but they seem to serenely be on their path.

Beings who admit the existence of a creator of all things, since all the particles of the universe are an integral part of that whole—that some call God and others call other things—are equal in essence, although in different evolutionary states along an immense trajectory, from being nothing to becoming immersed in the whole. They are capable of understanding the whole in the hopping about of a sparrow, in a colorful rosebud or in the dripping of water from the tap. They understand the vibration of universal intelligence in all its particles. They are beings who accept that God is in all forms of life, not contributing to the destruction of any of these forms, whatever the reason. They feel that the real relationship between the different particles of the whole is one of profound and supportive interconnection, of huge respect, of unconditional love.

They are beings who accept that all paths are possible and worthy of respect. They seek to make their path, concentrating their attention on that which is really useful for themselves, for others and for the whole. They do this in a way that is always constructive and serene, without demands, without certainties, but with the strong conviction of he who genuinely feels himself to be a particle of the whole. They are beings who do not feel inferior to whatever more or less revered entity, and who also do not feel superior to anyone at all.

They just feel. They are just equal to themselves, in the simplicity of being, but they keep constantly present the potential inherent to the whole.

They are beings who learn to elevate their thoughts, without reverence and without petulance, but using all available energy, in any position, in any place, whatever there is around them, come what may. They keep their thoughts positive and their actions constructive, seeking to do their part, with pleasure—not because they are obliged to, but for the pleasure of doing it, for the pleasure in being. And with love. They are beings who do not identify themselves as masters, nor do they consent to being called such, but who seek to assume irreprehensible conduct in thought, word and deed. They do not feel the necessity to brag, offend or humiliate; and they do not do it. They seek to fulfill; and they do.

For Agostinho da Silva (1988), a great thinker and firm believer in spirituality, the master is the man who does not order; he counsels and channels, pacifies and softens. It is not the word that sets fires, it is the word that revives the happy singing of the shepherd after the storm; he is not interested in winning, nor in getting to a good position; to become someone better—here is his entire program; for himself, the continuous blessing, humility and love for the other.

They are beings who live with the satisfaction of being truly useful and with the consciousness of duty done. Who give everything without asking for anything in return, and further, without accepting anything for themselves because after all they do not need it: they already have enough. They are beings who give, in their simplicity, their contribution to a better world.

To be simple has nothing to do with cultural or social standing; nor material wealth. The truly simple are not necessarily poor or uncultured, nor do they hide from normal life. They have sufficient firmness to feel equal to others at any time and in any place and always act with discernment. To be simple is to be unpretentious, available, capable, responsible and transparent, without needing evidence or praise. To be simple is to seek to live according to universal values, with a posture of spiritual peace; to seek the whole truth, accepting the possible truth.

Albert Einstein, Gandhi, Martin Luther King, Nelson Mandela, Mother Theresa of Calcutta, for example, were simple like many anonymous beings, from the most diverse races, from the most diverse social classes, from the most diverse cultures. To look serene, with a light smile, showing conviction in their principles and radiating positivity, those beings constantly maintain constructive positions, for the benefit of the whole. They are always available to serve superior interests, putting their own into second place. Truly simple people are those who create conditions for the construction of a better world, closer to the whole truth. Even if some do not do what falls to them, the simple will have the enormous fulfillment of doing their part, of giving their contribution, towards finding the whole truth.

• 27 •

Happiness

A CONSIDERABLE NUMBER OF PEOPLE live their lives in the pursuit of happiness, considering it to be a free right. They have the objective of being as happy as it is possible to be, which sometimes translates to a tendency for frequent overstimulation of the senses and/or the incessant desire for material possessions and/or power. But according to the dictionary, happiness is the satisfaction experienced by the individual upon managing to do what he was inclined to do or aspired to. And, while the satisfaction of desires is often easy, the realization of aspirations is usually hard, implying the development of some strength.

Thus, it seems we can enjoy various levels of happiness (Bruckner 2010). A first level is basically related to instinctive activity and to habits acquired through such activity. Some authors prefer the word pleasure to name the satisfaction found during a feast or in sexual acts. Some people seem to ignore the existence of other levels of happiness, seeking instead to experience situations of that kind very often, because the pleasure vanishes rapidly. They are people who give value to the accumulation of material wealth, which permits them to abundantly explore the stimulation of the senses. To this is added the pleasure of having, owning and the pleasure of being in charge of others, the pleasure of power, whether great or small, whether economic, political, organizational or any other kind. Sometimes, they enjoy only the pleasure of seeming to have or seeming to be in charge.

On the other hand, other people value the life of relationships, getting involved in emotions and passions and increasingly valuing feelings such as friendship and solidarity. The happiness they enjoy is naturally stronger and more durable, although intercut with moments of suffering, usually due to the bad use of their free will, as well as the natural deficiencies of relating to others, something that is common at our civilizational level. Often they give value to having, but also to being.

But there are human beings who also value intellectual life, seeking to stay informed, to think about what is happening and to find intelligent solutions. And the more they do it, the more they discover new levels of happiness, through the realization of ever more noble aspirations. They become more responsible people, valuing more and more the law of cause and effect, admitting that the more they try the better results they can achieve. The neuroscientist António Damásio believes that as societies evolve, we move towards greater harmony between the emotional and instinctive side and the rational and reflective side.

There also exist people who try to appropriately value the lives of instinct, relationships and intellect, looking for a harmonious control of the former by the latter, but having self-perfection as their aim. They understand that the best thing they can perfect in this world is themselves, focusing on this and becoming tolerant towards others. They desire to be equal to the best version possible of themselves, and make a constructive and constant effort in this direction. They are satisfied with little and understand that the more they have, the greater is the responsibility to properly manage what is, temporarily, theirs. These are the people who manage to be themselves, or to have a clear conscience for having done their duty. And, being at one with themselves, they tend to be at one with nature, creating conditions for the flow of suitable intuitions at the right times.

This last group is different from the others for the way in which they face everything in life. If the others love their ego above all, or some of the beings around them, they learn to respect the others, to respect universal values and, tuning into these values, learn or relearn to tune into the whole. They learn to unconditionally love the whole.

The life which they really value is the spiritual life, many of them believing themselves to be in just one more of their earthly lives. Some opt to isolate themselves from the world, to better self-analyze and purify, without outside influences. Others prefer to stay in contact with the civilizational reality, to better manage relationships (often very difficult ones) with third parties and/or to serve, which might be in a material or spiritual way. These people make an effort to progressively purify their thoughts, until they only want well-being for themselves, for all human beings, for all living creatures, for everything, for the whole. They constantly seek to control their words and their deeds, by keeping themselves constructive and genuinely useful to themselves and to everything around them, every day and every hour.

They seem to have the consciousness that they are still not perfect, while living tranquilly with the conviction of knowing how to tune in to the energy of superior characteristics, effectively channeling that energy, and they create conditions to realize their path of self-perfection. And they do it with simplicity and with the satisfaction of accomplishing their part. They know how to be and are at one with themselves anywhere, whoever they are with. They are demanding of themselves, respectful and tolerant of the others, staying firm in the defense of the great values and seeking to intelligently win over others so that they may discover the enormous pleasure of realizing their own path, but avoiding spending energy with them in vain.

They learn to not be upset by the actions of those who envy them, by those who slander or insult them, or by any form of being attacked. They defend themselves, avoiding bad situations and seeking to turn such situations into positive ones, always seeking to remain determinedly focused on accomplishing their objectives. They seek to desire only good, even for those who might want evil, conscious that everyone is always responsible for his own actions and understanding that the good of everyone contributes to the good of the whole. They understand and accept that greater happiness is not in the seeking of happiness, but in the making of happiness; it is not in the harvesting, but in the sowing; it is not in receiving but in giving. Serenity, self-confidence, balance in words and actions, composure, generosity, respect for everything and everyone, moderation, discipline, discretion, cordiality in treating others, the practice of good humor, integrity, constantly constructive orientation of thought, are qualities of he who lives happily.

On accepting themselves, serenely, as particles of the whole, linked with all the other particles, fearing nothing and nobody, nor even physical death, they find an enduring happiness. They are happy simply for accepting themselves as real particles of the universal whole, happy simply for existing in spiritual love.

• 28 •

Harmony

MANY OF US DESIRE AND DEMAND that the governments of our countries, and of all the others, find peaceful and democratic solutions for their countries, and, sometimes, we criticize them and other leaders because they cannot find the "obvious" paths to peace. However, if we, away from the big problems of the world, cannot keep our thoughts daily and constantly turned toward peace, how can we demand it of those who live swamped with questions of great importance and, often, with difficult solutions?

Not every one of us, ordinary citizens, can have a decisive word in the resolution of international crises. Nor should we expect to. What we can desire is, above all, that every one of us contributes his part. And in the case of world peace, it is important that everyone knows how to maintain their desire for peace twenty-four hours a day, through thoughts, words and deeds, beginning with inner peace. This will come about by everyone finding himself, tuning in to nature and to universal harmony; by making the effort to achieve peace at home, avoiding arguments with the ones we love, allowing them to be different and tolerating their defects, learning to build beautiful things together. By trying to get on with each other peacefully in the workplace, in the groups in which we participate, on public transport, on the street; by always respecting, and thus winning the right to be respected.

If everyone in the world, or at least a good majority of us, concentrate a bit of our attention to peace, seeking to build it from moment to moment, it will, sooner or later, become a reality. In our contact with nature, we find harmony in the mineral kingdom, the plant kingdom and in various animals. And when we seek to tune in to this universal harmony, we feel it crossing through everything, being beyond everything and being more than everything.

It seems that many human beings live their lives distracted, losing focus on reality, worrying about unimportant things or even things that are harmful to them and others; as if they forget the universal values; as if keeping atrophied their ability to connect to universal harmony. It seems that marvels of information from the senses confuse the meaning of human existence. It seems that, in many cases, the five senses stop being a window to the world, giving the capacity to human beings to better monitor their physical bodies and interact with their environments, and instead become a vehicle for illusions to prevail. It seems that most men tie themselves to a materialistic and mythological culture, self-limiting their capacity for understanding reality and living in accordance with a sophisticated set of precepts and prejudices. It seems that which cannot be expressed with words is not real and has no value, as if that which cannot be physically tested or experimented on does not exist.

But the abilities to reason and act with free will, which the human being has, always allow him to tune in to nature, live moments of lucidity, reconnect himself to eternal values through thoughts directed in a positive direction, and accept himself as a particle of peace, as a vehicle of love, as an active participant of the universal harmony. In any time and in any place, anyone can wind down, relax, abstract himself from the social whirl and tune in to nature, focusing his thoughts on what is positive, constructive, harmonious, lucid, crystalline. When the individual allows himself to expand his being to a wider field of consciousness, he will progressively identify with the universal harmony. And the more he integrates with that harmony, the less he is a part of the sea of cultural concepts: he accepts his identity more with collective evolution, and is less tied to the selfishness of an individual perspective. He loses his capacity for conflict and develops a natural ability to be in harmony, to be, in fact, a particle of harmony.

Harmony is the well-ordered placement of the parts of the

whole. Harmony is agreement. It is peace. It is friendship. It is pro-portion. It is conformity. It is coherence. It is, maybe, also equity, tolerance, availability, balance, confidence, fraternity, consideration, truth, love.

In Greek mythology, Harmony was the daughter of Zeus—the "supreme God, master of the lightning bolt, thunder and flame, who ruled the world"—and of Electra. But, according to Heracli-tus, "Beautiful harmony is born from contradictions and everything emerges from opposition." It seems, after all, to be something that emerges everywhere, which remains and endures. The disagree-ments, oppositions, conflicts, sooner or later, will end up in harmony.

Greek civilization thought of cosmic harmony as a "beautiful order in the Universe." And, in our time, we still find joy in universal harmony. When, at night, we sit serenely looking at the stars, we may feel small before the immensity of the universe, but we vibrate with all that infinite harmony. We also vibrate with the harmonious break of dawn on a spring day, the Earth waking up, translated in the cho-rus of birdsong and complemented by the beginning of the human's day of activity. Or watching the majestic sunset on hot summer days, putting the planet to bed. Universal harmony is omnipresent.

We feel this harmony when we hear the wind whistling through the trees of the forest, when we see the waves of the ocean kissing the sand, or when we feel the snow breaking up beneath our boots, while we wander through the mountains of some Nordic country. We feel it present in the swooping of the seagulls on land, announc-ing trouble at sea, on looking at the colors and shapes of tropical fish swimming calmly in their environment, in the delicate touch of a lioness on her cub, claws hidden in her paw, in the organized work of a swarm of bees in their hive, or the first cry of a newborn baby.

This harmony has always been and will always be. How-ever, sometimes, it seems we forget harmony and let ourselves get involved in disharmony, confusion and disturbance. Some more, others less, but all human beings, here or there, forget that the uni-verse is harmonious.

It might be said that less attentive individuals and less spiritually evolved have a lesser capacity for tuning in to universal harmony. And that, as we evolve spiritually, we become more attentive, more unified and more integrated into true life, with disharmony, confusion and disturbance repulsing us to the point where we merge ourselves with universal harmony. At that time, there will not exist any kind of repulsion. We will ourselves be harmony, wisdom, love. It may not be necessary to practice any kind of religious ritual for us to identify with universal harmony. It is here and in the whole universe. It exists now and forever.

Nature radiates harmony. We can tune into this harmony with our thoughts, with our words and attitudes. Serenely, we can also become shining beacons of universal harmony. It should be clear that we must not wait for our peers to transmit signals of harmony. Rather, we must feel ourselves to be permanently shining beacons of that harmony, able to resist any disharmony, confusion and disturbance that may come up in our way, or even collide with us. Safe in the knowledge that we are sowing harmony, we will reap it sooner or later or, in other words, we will win the right to enjoy it.

Universal harmony seems to be something that will remain beyond everything, and towards which each of us makes his journey until merging with it, fruit of his own spiritual merit. Thus, we feel equal in essence to all other human beings, although recognizing that we are at different stages on a vast trajectory. Each will thus be attentive to the peace that radiates from the serene gaze of some human beings from all social classes, races, ages or cultures, shining with an unmistakable interior peace. These men and women seem to enjoy genuine freedom, due to detachment from matter, probably based in a deep spiritual conviction. They are beings without fear who need nothing and who seem to live in harmony with universal laws.

Their perspective on life enables them to not fear losing anything, to not feel unhappy for not possessing, to not be scared of being unable to achieve this or that, to not envy those who show off what they believe they possess. In truth they are beings who do not possess; they only feel like temporary administrators, assuming the freedom of those who do not possess, the responsibility of those who administer, the authenticity of who is. They do not get upset when they see others doing what they believe to be incorrect, because they know to allow the others to enjoy their freedom, and they feel the responsibility to help them constructively, within their own limitations. They do not get angry when someone is rude because they do not need others to be pleasant to them.

They avoid those who seek to attack them. On the one hand, they know how to forgive their weaknesses; on the other, they do not want to harm them by allowing their incorrect practices. They behave with the serenity of one who is sure that he cannot be harmed, unless by himself (every time he takes a position that he later comes to regret). They know that they are responsible for their thoughts, for their words, for their attitudes. They avoid getting involved in situations that revolve around them. They assume the responsibility for their state of spirit and their experience of being.

This does not mean that an individual who lives in peace with himself strongly rejects material things, undervalues his body or wants to live in a bubble. On the contrary, with natural simplicity he enjoys the sensations of the physical world, with satisfaction, and not to satisfy frustrations or addictive situations. And he healthily shares his experiences, by desire not by obligation.

He seeks to care for his physical body as a way of keeping it an appropriate vehicle for material and, above all, spiritual success. He maintains a balanced and varied diet, avoiding ingesting and inhaling toxic substances, avoiding eating dead bodies, especially warm-blooded animals, such as mammals and fowls, and avoiding the excessive intake of fats and sugars. He does enough physical exercise to maintain his body in good condition, as well as to control the accumulation of fats and sugars. He maintains healthy contact with nature, seeking to breathe pure air and get some sunshine. He seeks to have restful sleep, in quality and quantity, creating conditions for mental serenity and tranquility of his conscience, providing him with pleasant and inspiring dreams.

These beings, who learn to live in harmony, are able to stay serene and constructively active, even in the most tragic times. In their thoughts, they keep the perspective of the whole. Their reasoning continues to follow a global logic. Their words and their attitudes serve the higher interests; those of the whole, but also their own.

Inner peace seems to be the only lever capable of raising world peace. This begins in every one of us. World peace is, after all, an individual issue. Looking at some beautiful examples, we might conclude that a change of circumstance is not necessary but, instead, a change of consciousness, or rather, a true tuning in to universal harmony.

• 29 •

Impersonal Life

IN RECENT YEARS, SOME THINKERS have defended the idea that during the 21st century the human being will modify his perspective of life and guide himself by other values. In *An Impersonal Life*, Joseph S. Benner describes how every one of us is in essence a particle of the universal whole, merely visiting planet Earth. Thus, he encourages the reader to think of himself as being that universal being (although only a particle), discovering his true interests in his conscience and finding himself in the simplicity of a particle of the whole, in service of the whole, through himself.

Benner (2017) points to a revitalization of material problems: "You are what you *believe* you are. Not one thing in your life is Real or has any value to you only as your *thinking* and *believing* has made it such" (73). With this perspective, the human being stops hyper-valuing material wealth. He does not see material resources as "his own," understanding himself as merely its loyal guardian for a limited time, according to his own ability to concentrate his attention, will and effort on them. Selfishness, unmeasured ambition and envy will lose meaning. Everything, after all, belongs to the whole.

He will naturally develop the notion of being useful to the whole. Once we understand that before anything we are the particle of the whole, through conscientious analysis of our way of being: how can we be truly useful to ourselves? And how can we be constructively useful to those around us, such as family, friends, neighbors, colleagues, acquaintances and strangers?

With a growing detachment from earthly things, the human

being will tend towards being concerned about being useful even to his enemies (who will then tend to become non-enemies) and, indiscriminately, to all the particles of the whole: humans, other animals, plants, minerals, and so, useful to the whole. Thus, the life of each of us will be less and less characterized by "our" things, a life ever more impersonal.

The notion of charity will cease to have any meaning. Everything belongs to everybody. Each one has only temporarily available the part that he deserves, or needs, for his evolutionary process. The notion of solidarity will become stronger (harmonious, discreet, crystalline). Everything belongs to everybody. And everybody mutually supports everybody else, always.

Reading authors like Benner seems to help us to abstract ourselves from ordinary things of our day-to-day lives and dive into the ideal and what appears to be unreal. But, after all, it seems that living in love with ordinary things of our day-to-day lives is what brought us to a life far from the ideal and, in that way, truly unreal.

Another author, Ken Carey (1991), in his book *Starseed: The Third Millennium*, expresses it like this: "The replication of another generation in the image of the former is no longer possible. The current generation of young will drink but shallow draughts at the fount of illusion, if they drink at all. For the perceptive of your race have felt the changing climate of the world. And they have realized that in this new climate generational duplication would not perpetuate their societies but terminate them" (109).

In the last few decades, the world has evolved at an accelerated rhythm in various ways, especially from an educational point of view. Despite this, there are still many people who live lives based on what they believe their parents would like them to do, just as there are an enormous number of citizens who orient their lives based on the structured understanding and beliefs of other human beings, within frames of preconceptions of social, religious, and political organizations.

We consider advantageous to respect parents, hear their ideas, suggestions, advice, consider their options and attitudes. But it should be the self, the adult self, that decides the direction for his life. As good listeners, we should intuit between words, sensing the essence of the spirit behind what the others tell us. However, in the end, we should decide in accordance with our conscience, without fear, assuming all our dimensions, immersed in the love which illuminates creativity and life.

More and more, the human being feels the duty to seek the truth that lies behind each ritual, each idea, each ceremony found in huge variety in the multiple expressions of that truth. He feels that he should be grateful to those who seek to show him their perspective on reality. But, in the end, he feels that the meaning of his life should spring from inside, discovering his truth, using his own capacity to channel available energy to illuminate his way, in the construction of a better world. Thanks to the more liberal kinds of education in the last few decades, many youths today understand that orienting their lives around human organizations will bring them little fulfillment and almost no happiness. Thus, there are a growing number of people who seek the maximum information, to analyze and decide for themselves, in accordance with their understanding of the universe.

The building of a new era of peace and harmony may be able to be realized when each human understands that he must not limit himself to the study of already known spiritual things. It will be good to always be open to new ideas, hear different points of view, obtain a great deal of information, but never allow anyone to make one doubt oneself. Then, the spiritual reality will emerge from the core of everyone. It is thus that each one understands who he is and what his real dimension is, in the whole.

Patterns of identity centered on the individual and materiality, apparently generators of fears, limitations and frustrations, seem to evaporate progressively. There are beings who stand out, in a simple way, calmly, who emerge from the most diverse social classes, different races and nationalities, who seem to allow other dimensions of eternity penetrate them, silently, when they take on board that they are particles of the whole. They are recognized by their serene posture, their great sensitivity, the independence of their movements, the natural nobility of their attitudes, their great creativity, or the personal sense of security held up by the humility of he who lives through love. Citing Carey again: "Healthy human individuality brings with it a *hologrammatic* understanding of the Being whose unfoldment is this universe, *an understanding in which the whole is microcosmically reflected in the structure of the part*" (25).

In the flow of an existence, there are profoundly remarkable moments which lead us to change the direction in which we lead our lives. They are moments in which (sometimes unexpected, sometimes less so) something happens that make us absorb a significant meaning, seeming to qualitatively alter our psychophysiological structure and compelling us to higher leaps. An accident happens to a family member or to us, or we read a book, or we just hear a sentence uttered to us by someone. We meet someone or something which leaves a strong impression. While in certain cases we have the feeling that we have already met that person in another time, or we already knew something that we only just thought of, these occurrences are no less striking.

When we live through these situations, we become physically and mentally shaken, and available to other vibrations, like someone acquiring another level of consciousness of himself and of the universe. With more or less amazement, we seem to discover ourselves and wake to new levels of reality. We have the feeling that everything always was, that everything was there already, just that we hadn't understood it, hadn't got there yet; our attention was concentrated on other things which seemed to obscure what we discovered now. As if we didn't want to see what was in front of us, to understand the obvious.

They are moments of extraordinary beauty not because the universe is changing, but because we have made the necessary journey to get there, because we have conquered the right to go beyond, because we have been able to be open to change, recognizing our limitations and our ignorance. This is a beauty which is in us, in our progression, in our encounter with the knowledge that comes from within and without, which penetrates us, like all the rest. Suddenly, we have an unshakeable certainty. We don't mind if it is in books. We don't care if it was whispered to us or intuited. We feel ourselves in tune with reality; with other levels of reality. We are more mature, perhaps more evolved. We feel well and motivated to continue to grow, having the necessary insight to continue on our path, always equal and always different to all other paths.

The path is one of experimentation, of realization, of discovery, of integration. A path of small but dazzling illuminations. An individual path, but deeply interconnected with everyone and everything. A path of learning but also of growing mastery. A path that seems to bring us closer to the whole, since the more we feel we are one of its particles, the more we feel the whole in ourselves. The path is the discovery of ourselves, of getting to know ourselves, in a crescendo of humility, of stripping down, of truly integrated participation. Waking up to reality, to what is as simple as it is.

We understand that our path is to be walked by us, under our own steam. Without political protection, without the benefits of faith, without miraculous solutions, because all of this would be against universal justice. We cultivate the family unit, values of friendship and solidarity, the capacity to function in a group; but assuming the direction of our path, in a responsible manner, not waiting for the others to do what we are supposed to do. We feel the necessity to perfect ourselves, to correct ourselves, to be better and better, conscious that for this we need to develop constructive work. We feel the necessity to head in the direction of a more complete knowledge of things, of universal wisdom.

Assuming the truth, the need to hide feelings disappears, the soul expressing itself freely through thoughts, words and actions. Assuming the meaning of universal unity, selfishness and the materialistic, immediatist perspective fall away, and the satisfaction of sharing honestly stands out, in the search for real benefits for the self, for others, for the whole. It seems that not many words are necessary. The transparency of our thoughts is captured by others and we easily sense the characteristics of the environment around us and the direction of will of those who surround us.

We learn to observe fully, reading between the lines and understanding what really works to our advantage, and to that of others and of the whole; or rather, keeping respect for universal harmony. These are notions which transcend those of sin and of right and wrong, of which, after all, there are plenty. In this way, it doesn't make sense to damage or destroy anything, but just construct. We learn to develop a mutually dependent relationship with the environment, conscious that every cause corresponds to an effect and every effect has its cause. Conflict or war are no longer options.

It becomes unthinkable to smoke carcinogens and drink liquids that impede the function of our nervous system. The advantages are clear in a life in contact with nature, tuned in to its laws, immutable laws which encompass everything. Simplicity emerges naturally when we stop worrying about appearances and start just being, from our behavior to what we wrap ourselves in, whether that is our clothes or our habitation.

Education becomes an effective, constructive support from more experienced people—parents, grandparents, professional educators—always based in example, because teaching something cannot result from practicing the opposite. And, as the education of a people is also done by what some communicate to others, the media, social communication, becomes something positive, seeking valuable happenings and putting away images of behaviors to avoid, conscientiously, honestly, responsibly. Not by being prohibited, but by free choice of spectators and broadcasters.

Professional activities are carried out with happiness and commitment, in environments of good camaraderie and where employers and employees try to put together the necessary conditions for the success of all. Individual and collective competence is naturally accomplished. There will be no sense in overpaying professional sportspeople and film actors, while teachers and researchers become well paid. Society recognizes its most valued members and, among them, the most apt are selected to serve the collective in the exercise of governance, this being serene, impartial and efficient.

Thus, the human being will contribute to building a more evolved world, without worrying why so many seem to have forgotten to realize it. But having the certainty of what is worth enjoying as part of the inebriating pleasure of taking part in universal harmony.

♦ 30 ♦

Unconditional Love

THERE ARE THOSE WHO USE A sheet of paper to help a centipede that entered the house to get back into the garden. There are those who use a stick to help a snake get out of the swimming pool it has fallen into. We see people who systematically feed stray cats. These are small examples of those who respect life in its most diverse forms, not feeling the necessity to step on or crush living creatures they consider less evolved or less important. It seems that human beings have developed a growing respect and a greater sense of solidarity among them.

Goodwill is considered a virtue, and support systems have evolved, from a more evident system of charities incentivizing indolence and laziness, to more discreet actions of helping others to free themselves from problems, by learning to overcome them with their own effort. There currently exist a large number of people who support others with attention, a sense of usefulness and the spirit of abnegation, helping vulnerable children, the elderly, the poor, the infirm, promoting the recovery of addicts and offenders, or simply helping people in trouble, whether family, friend, stranger or even enemy. The true humanist is disinterested, neither asking nor accepting anything for his help, which is done simply for love of the others.

Each human being is increasingly recognizing himself as a particle of the whole and understanding that happiness is found in what he constructively achieves in favor of the whole, initially by being useful to himself, then to family and friends, then to humanity in general, and then to the whole. Solidarity provides radiant, contagious happiness that promotes material progress but, above all, spiritual progress.

We can say that selfishness will give way to humanitarianism, and after that, to universalism. The growing respect for the whole and all its particles brings human beings to reduce the unbalanced destruction of animal and plant life. The wake-up call for universal harmony leads them to progressively allow other beings to live and support that life in all its forms. A considerable number of people already accept that all beings, even the weakest and unprotected, deserve our attention, our respect and our solidarity.

Animals, usually considered irrational in the evolutionary phase in which they find themselves, generally have a naturally pure and defenseless posture, allowing us to develop some kind of communication with them, of a subjective nature, which is sometimes intense and long lasting, in some cases even with strong affectionate connections. As people develop their emotional abilities and empathy to the pain of others, they end attitudes of cruelty to animals, which probably, with time, will tend to disappear.

The arbitrary and keenly selfish practice of the destruction of vegetable species, too, is increasingly criticized and slowly being abandoned. Ecological and environmental movements fight against this gratuitous destruction. A growing spirit of respect, tolerance and solidarity, or in other words, of love for all particles of the universe, emerges.

Tolerance is knowing how to accept other ways of thinking, of expressing oneself or of acting; it is knowing to accept that which we understand to be the errors of others and to forgive or pardon them; it is leniency. It implies respect for others, accepting that they are as they are, do what they know how to do, in accordance with their evolutionary level. Respect for the freedom of others, within reasonable limits, or rather, while the use of that freedom does not disturb our own freedom or that of others. It translates as understanding for others, not wanting to force them to be perfect; as well as having the patience to put up with their imperfections, we also want them to put up with ours. It is built with consideration, discipline and self-control, seeking to control our own impulses, even if they are well-intentioned.

Tolerance implies the courage to confront situations with which we disagree, without trying to manipulate or destroy them, but also without abdicating the points of view that, thoughtfully, we consider more, better or truly evolved. Further, it implies a spirit of renouncing the improper use of available energy, seeking to channel it appropriately, through well-directed thoughts, words of advice or constructive and exemplary attitudes; springing always from acceptance, before incentivizing the transformation. Tolerance reveals the self-confidence of one who feels that he chooses the path he walks, without needing to impose on others, nor convince them of the advantages of choosing the same path, but rather giving them the space and time to make their own choices, accepting that evolution is not made in leaps, but step by step, progressively; and by gaining it for oneself, not by imposing it on others.

It is developed in fraternity and depending on the degree of spirituality. Remember how religions like Christianity and Judaism were persecuted in the early centuries of our era, while from the year 380 onwards, Christianity became the only accepted religion in most European countries. Religious intolerance developed in Catholicism, reaching its height with the Inquisition. Only in the last few centuries, with influence from various thinkers, religious freedom came to be accepted, being finally proclaimed in the Universal Declaration of Human Rights, by the United Nations, in 1948.

Tolerance is, in a way, kindness, while it should not be permissiveness or connivance. To be tolerant is to be good, not to be nice; it is to be attentive, available, positive, constructive or even enterprising. It is to be firm in what is essential, but flexible in the rest. Tolerance is wisdom. It transcends the materialism of things, being one of the universal values. Tolerance is love. It is to love others as one loves oneself, to love the whole more than others or oneself.

At its best, the perfect human being will love all other beings, even the less evolved. At its best, the perfect being will love all the other animals, even those who—living in their more primal state of instinctive life—are dangerous. At its best, the perfect being will love the whole cosmos; it will love the whole. To love the whole is to have the capacity to love even those who take the role of enemy.

To love the whole is to even love the unspeakable terrorist who cannot be forced to change; but the temporary interruption of his freedom, made with persuasion and love, may contribute towards his journey of self-correction. When Jesus said, "Love your enemies," he probably wanted to alert humanity to the need to fill this requirement in the path of spiritual learning. It may be the last step of this path but, without doubt, it is a necessary step.

The splendor of universal realization is in love. And to love is to keep constructively trying to achieve the best for oneself, for the others—even for those who want to attack us—and for all. To love is to succeed at keeping thoughts directed towards one's major objectives, without letting oneself be tripped up or diverted, whatever happens. Through serenity and effectiveness of attitude, the human being is able to win the respect and admiration of others, even of those who wish him ill or to attack him. And, if this is not the case, he is able to have patience: we are responsible for what we do, not for what the others do.

The human being that feels the pleasure in having always positive thoughts creates conditions to always act constructively and to naturally seek harmonious positions. He thus develops love for himself and for the others, increasingly, without conditions or restrictions. In this way, sooner or later, he will also be loved without conditions or restrictions. When he, in fact, loves all the particles of the whole, he will be profoundly integrated in it. He will be only love. He will be, really and definitively, a particle of universal love.

Bibliography

A

Achterberg, J., Cooke, K., Richards, T., Standish, L., Kozak, L., and Lake, J. (2005). Evidence for correlations between distant intentionality and brain function in recipients. *Journal of Alternative and Complementary Medicine* 11(6): 965–971.

Acunzo, D., Evrard, R., and Rebeyron, T. (2013). Anomalous experiences, psi and functional neuroimaging. *Frontiers in Human Neuroscience* 7: 893. DOI: https://doi.org/10.3389/fnhum.2013.00893.

Aïvanhov, O. M. (1983). *A luz, espírito vivo.* Lisbon, Portugal: Prosveta.

Alarcão, Z., and Fonseca, J. (2016). The effect of Reiki therapy on quality of life of patient with blood cancer: Results from a randomized controlled trial. *European Journal of Integrative Medicine* 8: 239–249. DOI: https://doi.org/10.1016/j.eujim.2015.12.003.

Alexander, E. (2012). *Proof of heaven: A neurosurgeon's journey into the afterlife.* New York: Simon & Schuster Paperback.

Almeder, R. (1992). *Death and personal survival: The evidence for life after death.* Lanham, MD: Rowman & Littlefield.

Alvarado, C. (2011). Eusapia Palladino: An autobiographical essay. *Journal of Scientific Exploration* 25(1): 77–101.

Alvarado, C., and Zingrone, N. (1994). Individual differences in aura vision: Relationships to visual imagery and imaginative-fantasy experiences. *European Journal of Parapsychology* 10: 1–30.

Ambach, W. (2008). Correlations between the EEGs of two spatially separated subjects—a replication study. *European Journal of Parapsychology* 23(2): 131–146.

Andrade, H. (2001). *Psi quântico.* Votuporanga, SP: Casa Editora Espírita Pierre Paul Didier.

Andrews, T. (1994). *Como ver e interpretar a aura.* 2nd ed. São Paulo: Siciliano.

Assefi, N., Bogart, A., Goldberg, J., and Buchwald, D. (2008). Reiki for the treatment of fibromyalgia: A randomized controlled trial. *Journal of Alternative and Complementary Medicine* 14(9): 1115–1122. DOI: https://doi.org/10.1089/acm.2008.0068.

Aurobindo, S. (1970). *The life divine.* Pondicherry, India: Sri Aurobindo Ashram Trust.

_____. (1976). *The synthesis of yoga.* 6th ed. Pondicherry, India: Sri Aurobindo Ashram Trust.

Bibliography

B

Baldwin, A. L., Wagers, C., and Schwartz, G. E. (2008). Reiki improves heart rate homeostasis in laboratory rats. *Journal of Alternative and Complementary Medicine* 14(4): 417–422. DOI: https://doi.org/10.1089/acm.2007.0753.

Bancel, P. (2017). Searching for global consciousness: A 17-year exploration. *Explore: The Journal of Science and Healing* 13(2): 94–101. DOI: https://doi.org/10.1016/j.explore.2016.12.003.

Bancel, P., and Nelson, R. (2008). The GCP event experiment: Design, analytical methods, results. *Journal of Scientific Exploration* 22(3): 259–269.

Barbeau, E., Wendling, F., Régis, J., Duncan, R., Poncet, M., Chauvel, P., and Bartolomei, F. (2005). Recollection of vivid memories after periorbital region stimulations: Synchronization in the theta range of spatially distributed brain areas. *Neuropsychologia* 43(9): 1329–1337.

Bartolomei, F., Barbeau, E., Gavaret, M., Guye, M., McGonigal, A., Régis, J., and Chauvel, P. (2004). Cortical stimulation study of the role of rhinal cortex in déjà vu and reminiscence of memories. *Neurology* 63(5): 858–864.

Bayless, R. (1959). Correspondence. *Journal of the American Society for Psychical Research* 53: 35–39.

Beauregard, M., Courtemanche, J., and Paquette, V. (2009). Brain activity in near-death experiences during a meditative state. *Resuscitation* 80. DOI: https://doi.org/10.1016/j.resuscitation.2009.05.006.

Beauregard, M. and O'Leary, D. (2007). *The spiritual brain: A neuroscientist's case for the existence of the soul.* New York: HarperOne.

Beauregard, M., Schwartz, G. E., Miller, L., Dossey, L., Moreira-Almeida, A., Schlitz, M., Sheldrake, R., and Tart, C. (2014). Manifesto for a post-materialist science. *Explore: The Journal of Science and Healing* 10(5): 272–274. DOI: https://doi.org/10.1016/j.explore.2014.06.008.

Beischel J. (2007). Contemporary methods used in laboratory-based mediumship research. *Journal of Parapsychology* 71: 37–68.

Beischel, J., Boccuzzi, M., Biuso, M., and Rock, A. J. (2015). Anomalous information reception by research mediums under blinded conditions II: Replication and extension. *Explore: The Journal of Science and Healing* 11(2): 136–142. DOI: https://doi.org/10.1016/j.explore.2015.01.001.

Beischel, J., and Schwartz, G. (2007). Anomalous information reception by research mediums demonstrated using a novel triple-blind protocol. *Explore: The Journal of Science and Healing* 3(1): 23–27. DOI: https://doi.org/10.1016/j.explore.2006.10.004.

Belanti, J., Perera, M., and Jagadheesan, K. (2008). Phenomenology of near-death experiences: A cross-cultural perspective. *Transcultural Psychiatry* 45(1): 121–133. DOI: https://doi.org/10.1177/1363461507088001.

Bem, D. (2005). Review of book "The afterlife experiments: Breakthrough scientific evidence of life after death" by Gary E. Schwartz. *Journal of Parapsychology* 69: 173–183.

Bem, D., and Honorton, C. (1994). Does psi exist? Replicable evidence for an anomalous process of information transfer. *Psychological Bulletin* 115: 4–18.

Benner, J. S. (2017). *The impersonal life: The classic of self-realization.* New York: TarcherPerigee.

Benor, D. (2007). *Healing research: Volume I (popular edition). Spiritual healing: Scientific validation of a healing revolution.* Bellmawr, NJ: Wholistic Healing.

Bibliography

Besant, A. (1917). *Man and his bodies*. Los Angeles: Theosophical.

_____. (1995). *Um estudo sobre a consciência*. São Paulo: Pensamento.

Besant, A., and Leadbeater, C. W. (1901). *Thought forms*. London: Theosophical.

Bettis, W. (1998). Researching past lives: Facts or subjective experience? *The Journal of Regression Therapy* 12(1):54–62.

Bierman, D. J., and Scholte, H. S. (2002). A fMRI brain imaging study of presentiment. *Journal of International Society of Life Information Science* 20(2): 380–389.

Blackmore, S. (1993). *Experiências fora do corpo*. São Paulo: Pensamento.

_____. (2003). Consciousness: An introduction. London: Hodder and Stoughton.

Blanke, O., Landis, T., Spinelli, L., and Seeck, M. (2004). Out-of-body experience and autoscopy of neurological origins. *Brain* 127(2): 243–258.

Blavatsky, H. P. (1979). *The secret doctrine*. Pasadena, CA: Theosophical University Press.

Bowman, C. (1998). *Children's past lives—How past lives memories affect your child*. New York: Bantam.

Braithwaite, J. J., Broglia, E., Bagshaw, A. P., and Wilkins, A. J. (2013). Evidence for elevated cortical hyperexcitability and its association with out-of-body experiences in the non-clinical population: New findings from a pattern-glare task. *Cortex* 49(3): 793–805. DOI: https://doi.org/10.1016/j.cortex.2011.11.013.

Braud, W. (2002). Psi-favorable conditions. In *New frontiers of human science*, ed. V. G. Rammohan (Jefferson, NC: McFarland), 95–118.

Braude, S. (2003). *Immortal Remains—The evidence for life after death*. Boston: Rowman & Littlefield.

_____. (2007). *The gold leaf lady and other parapsychological investigations*. Chicago: University of Chicago Press.

_____. (2015). Macro-psychokinesis. In *Parapsychology: A handbook for the 21st century*, ed. E. Cardeña, J. Palmer and D. Marcusson-Clavertz (Jefferson, NC: McFarland), 266–281.

Broughton, R. S., and Alexander, C. H. (1997). Autoganzfeld II: An attempted replication of the PRL ganzfeld research. *Journal of Parapsychology* 61: 209–226.

Bruckner, P. (2010). *Perpetual euphoria: On the duty to be happy*. Princeton: Princeton University Press.

Brune, F., and Chauvin, R. (1994). *Linha direta do Além. Transcomunicação instrumental: realidade ou utopia?* Sobradinho, Brazil: Edicel.

Bruno, G. (1984). *Acerca do infinito, do universo e dos mundos*. Lisbon: Fundação Calouste Gulbenkian.

Butler, T. (2012). EVP using VoIP and telephones. *Association TransCommunication News Journal* 31(3): 5–6.

Byrd, R. (1988). Positive therapeutic effects of intercessory prayer in a coronary care unit population. *Southern Medical Journal* 81(7): 826–829.

C

Cardeña, E. (2013). Eminent authors from other areas. *Mindfield* 5: 83–90.

_____. (2014). A call for an open, informed study of all aspects of consciousness. *Frontiers in Human Neuroscience* 8: 17. DOI: https://doi.org/10.3389/fnhum.2014.00017.

Cardeña, E., Lynn, S. J., and Krippner, S. (2000). *Varieties of anomalous experiences: Examining the scientific evidence*. Washington, DC: American Psychological Association.

Bibliography

Cardoso, A. (2010). *Electronic voices: Contact with another dimension.* Winchester, UK: O-Books.

_____. (2012). A two-year investigation of the allegedly anomalous electronic voices or EVP. *NeuroQuantology* 10(3): 492–514.

_____. (2017). *Electronic contact with the dead—What do the voices tell us?* Hove, UK: White Crow.

Carey, K. (1991). *Starseed. The third millennium: Living in the posthistoric world.* San Francisco: HarperCollins.

Carpenter, J. C. (2012). *First Sight—ESP and parapsychology in everyday life.* Plymouth, UK: Rowman & Littlefield.

Cetin, B. (1999). *Energía Universal: una Investigación Sistemática y Científica.* Mexico: Author.

Charland-Verville, V., Jourdan, J.-P., Thonnard, M., Ledoux, D., Donneau, A.-F., Quertemont, E., and Laureys, S. (2014). Near-death experiences in non-life-threatening events and coma of different etiologies. *Frontiers in Human Neuroscience* 8: 203. DOI: https://doi.org/10.3389/fnhum.2014.00203.

Charman, R. (2006). Has direct brain to brain communication been demonstrated by electroencephalographic monitoring of paired or group subjects? *Journal Society for Psychical Research* 70(882): 1–24.

Chaudhuri, H. (1965). *Integral yoga.* London: Allen & Unwin.

Chauvin, R. (1986). A PK experiment with mice. *Journal of the Society for Psychical Research* 53: 348–351.

Chéroux, C., Fischer, A., Apraxine, P., Canguilhem, D., and Schmidt, S. (2004). *The perfect medium—Photography and the occult.* New Haven, CT: Yale University Press.

Clark, R. L. (1995). *Past-life therapy: The state of the art.* Austin, TX: Rising Star.

_____. (1997). A new understanding of reincarnation through past-life recall. *The Journal of Regression Therapy* 11(1): 55–62.

Collerton, D., Perry, E., and McKeith, I. (2005). Why people see things that are not there: A novel perception and attention deficit model for recurrent complex visual hallucinations. *Behavioral and Brain Sciences* 28(6): 737–757.

Collins, M. (1952). *The idyll of the white lotus.* Adyar, India: Theosophical.

Costa, V. (2012). *A nova consciência universal.* Lisbon: Author.

Covey, S. R. (1999). *Living the 7 habits: Stories of courage and inspiration.* New York: Simon & Schuster.

Crawford, C., Sparber, A., and Jonas, W. (2003). A systematic review of the quality of research on hands-on and distance healing: Clinical and laboratory studies. *Alternative Therapies* 9(3 suppl.): A96–104.

Creath, K., and Schwartz, G. (2004). Measuring effects of music, noise, and healing energy using a seed germination bioassay. *The Journal of Alternative and Complementary Medicine* 10(1): 113–122.

Currie, I. (1998). *Visions of immortality: The incredible findings of a century of research on death.* Rockport, MA: Element.

D

Damásio, A. (2010). *O livro da consciência.* Lisbon: Círculo de Leitores.

_____. (2017). *A estranha ordem das coisas: A vida, os sentimentos e as culturas humanas.* Lisbon: Círculo de Leitores.

Darnell, S. (1979). *Voces sin rostro.* Barcelona: Petronio.

Bibliography

Decaix, R., and Labroille, C. (1995). *Dispositif de mesure des energies vibratoires emises para la matiere.* French Patent No. FR2710745 (A1). Paris: Institut National de la Propriété Industrielle.

De' Carli, J. (2009). *Amor, saúde e transformação.* Lisbon: Dinalivro.

Delgado, J. M. (1995). *El control de la mente.* Madrid: Espasa-Calpe.

Delorme, A., Beischel, J., Michel, L., Boccuzzi, M., Radin, D., and Mills, P. (2013). Electrocortical activity associated with subjective communication with the deceased. *Frontiers in Psychology* 4: 834.

Descamps, M. A., Alfilé, L., and Nicolescu, B. (1997). *O que é o Transpessoal?* Lisbon: Temática.

Dethlefsen, T. (1976). *A regressão a vidas passadas como método de cura.* São Paulo: Pensamento.

Dossey, L. (1993). *Healing words: The power of prayer and the practice of medicine.* San Francisco: Harper.

_____. (2013). *One Mind: How our individual mind is part of a greater consciousness and why it matters.* USA: Hay House.

_____. (2014). Spirituality and nonlocal mind: A necessary dyad. *Spirituality in Clinical Practice* 1(1): 29–42. DOI: https://doi.org/10.1037/scp0000001.

Drouot, P. (1996). *Somos todos imortais.* Rio de Janeiro: Nova Era.

Duane, T. D., and Behrendt, T. (1965). Extrasensory electroencephalographic induction between identical twins. *Science* 150(3694): 367. DOI: https://doi.org/10.1126/science.150.3694.367.

Duerden, T. (2004). An aura of confusion. Part 2: The aided eye—"imaging the aura?" *Complementary Therapies in Nursing and Midwifery* 10: 116–123.

Dunne, B. and Jahn, R. (2005). Consciousness, information and living systems. *Cellular and Molecular Biology* 51: 703–714.

Dutton, D., and Williams, C. (2009). Clever beasts and faithful pets: A critical review of animal psi research. *Journal of Parapsychology* 73(1): 43–70.

E

Easton, S., Blake, O., and Mohr, C. (2009). A putative implication for fronto-parietal connectivity in out-of-body experiences. *Cortex* 45(2): 216–227.

Eckartshausen, K. V. (2003). *Algumas palavras do mais profundo do ser.* São Paulo: Rosacruz.

Ehrsson, H. H. (2007). The experimental induction of out-of-body experiences. *Science* 317(5841): 1048.

Einstein, A. (2007). *The world as I see it.* San Diego, CA: Book Tree.

Eisenberg, H., and Donderi, D. (1979). Telepathic transfer of emotional information in humans. *Journal of Psychology* 103: 19–43.

Eisenbud, J. (1989). *The world of Ted Serios.* 2nd ed. Jefferson, NC: McFarland.

Evans-Wentz, W. Y. (1993). *O livro tibetano dos mortos.* São Paulo: Pensamento.

F

Facco, E., and Agrillo, C. (2012). Near-death-like experiences without life-threatening conditions or brain disorders: A hypothesis from a case report. *Frontiers in Psychology* 3: 490. DOI: https://doi.org/10.3389/fpsyg.2012.00490.

Bibliography

Fenwick, P. (1996). Chickens don't lie. *Network: The Scientific and Medical Network Revue* 62: 12–13.

Fenwick, P., and Fenwick, E. (2008). *The art of dying.* London: Continuum.

Fontana, D. (2006). *Is there an afterlife?* London: Iff.

Freedman, T. B. (2002). *Soul echoes: The healing power of past-life therapy.* New York: Citadel.

French, C. C. (2003). Fantastic memories: The relevance of research into eyewitness testimony and false memories for reports of anomalous experiences. *Journal of Consciousness Studies* 10(6–7), 153–174.

G

Gabbard, G. O., and Twemlow, S. W. (1991). Do "near-death experiences" occur only near death?—Revisited. *Journal of Near-Death Studies* 10(1): 41–47. DOI: https://doi.org/10.1007/bf01073295.

Gandhi, M. (1999). *Preceitos de vida.* Lisbon: Pergaminho.

Gauld, A., and Cornell, T. (1979). *Poltergeists.* London: Routledge & Kegan Paul.

Godoy, H. (2002). *Terapia da Regressão—teoria e técnicas.* São Paulo: Cultrix.

Goswami, A. (2005). *A física da alma.* São Paulo: Aleph.

Govinda, L. (1959). *Foundations of Tibetan mysticism.* London. Rider.

Grad, B. (1976). The biological effects of the "laying on of hands" on animals and plants: Implications for biology. In *Parapsychology: Its relations to physics, biology, psychology and psychiatry,* ed. G. R. Schmeidler (Metuchen, NJ: Scarecrow), 76–89.

Green, M. B., Ooguri, H., and Schwarz, J. H. (2007). Nondecoupling of maximal supergravity from the superstring. *Physical Review Letters* 99(4): 041601.

Green, M. B., and Schwarz, J. H. (1984a). Superstring field theory. *Nuclear Physics* 243(3, section B): 475–536. DOI: https://doi.org/10.1016/0550-3213(84)90488-7.

_____. (1984b). The structure of superstring field theories. *Physics Letters B* 140(1–2), 33–38. DOI: https://doi.org/10.1016/0370-2693(84)91041-4.

Green, M. B., Schwarz, J. H., and Witten, E. (2012a). *Superstring theory.* Vol. 1. *Introduction.* Cambridge, UK: Cambridge University Press.

_____. (2012b). *Superstring theory.* Vol. 2. *Loop amplitudes, anomalies and phenomenology.* Cambridge, UK: Cambridge University Press.

Greene, B. (2004). *O universo elegante.* Lisbon: Gradiva.

Greyson, B. (1983). The near-death experience scale: Construction, reliability, and validity. *The Journal of Nervous and Mental Disease* 171(6): 369–375.

_____. (1993). Varieties of near-death experience. *Psychiatry* 56: 390–99.

_____. (2003). Incidence and correlates of near-death experiences in a cardiac care unit. *General Hospital Psychiatry* 25(4): 269–276. DOI: https://doi.org/10.1016/S0163-8343(03)00042-2.

_____. (2015). Western scientific approaches to near-death experiences. *Humanities* 4(4): 775.

Grinberg-Zylberbaum, J., Delaflor, M., Attie, L., and Goswami, L. (1994). The Einstein-Podolsky-Rosen paradox in the brain: The transferred potential. *Physics Essays* 7(4): 422–428.

Groth-Marnat, G., and Summers, R. (1998). Altered beliefs, attitudes, and behaviors following near-death experiences. *Journal of Humanistic Psychology* 38: 110–125.

Guedes, A. P. (1983). *Ciência espírita.* 7th ed. Rio de Janeiro: Centro Redentor.

H

Haraldsson, E. (1995). Personality and abilities of children claiming previous-life memories. *Journal of Nervous and Mental Disease* 183: 445–451.

_____. (1997). A psychological comparison between ordinary children and those who claim previous-life memories. *Journal of Scientific Exploration* 11: 323–335.

_____. (2000). Birthmarks and claims of previous-life memories. *Journal of the Society for Psychical Research* 64: 16–25.

_____. (2003). Children who speak of past-life experience: Is there a psychological explanation? *Psychology and Psychotherapy: Theory Research and Practice* 76: 55–67.

_____. (2010). *The departed among the living: An investigative study of afterlife encounters.* Guilford, UK: White Crow.

Haraldsson, E., and Houtkooper, J. M. (1991). Psychic experiences in the multinational human values study: Who reports them? *The Journal of the American Society for Psychical Research* 85(2): 145–165.

Harari, Y. N. (2017). *Sapiens: História breve da humanidade.* 6th ed. Amadora, Portugal: Elsinore.

Hart, H. (1954). ESP projection: Spontaneous cases and the experimental method. *Journal of the American Society for Psychical Research* 48: 121–146.

_____. (1967). Scientific survival research. *International Journal of Parapsychology* 9: 43–52.

Hart, L. K., Freel, M., Haylock, P., and Lutgendorf, S. (2011). The use of healing touch in integrative oncology. *Clinical Journal of Oncology Nursing* 15(5): 519–525. DOI: https://doi.org/10.1188/11.CJON.519-525.

Hearne, K. (1981). Visually evoked responses and ESP: Failure to replicate previous findings. *Journal of the Society of Psychic Research* 51: 145–147.

Hell, D. (2005). Medicina sem alma? *Revista da Ordem dos Médicos* 63: 54–59.

Houran, J., and Lange, R. (2001). *Hauntings and poltergeists: multidisciplinary perspectives.* Jefferson, NC: McFarland.

I

Irwin, H., and Watt, C. (2007). *An introduction to parapsychology.* Jefferson, NC: McFarland.

J

Jahn, R. G., Dunne, B, Nelson, R., Dobyns, Y. and Bradish, G. (1997). Correlations of random binary sequences with pre-stated operator intention: A review of a 12 year program. *Journal of Scientific Exploration* 11(3): 345–367.

Jensen, C. G., and Cardeña, E. (2009). A controlled long-distance test of a professional medium. *European Journal of Parapsychology* 24: 53–67.

Jesus, F. A. (1973). *Trajetória evolutiva.* 5th ed. Rio de Janeiro: Centro Redentor.

Bibliography

Johnson, M. (1989). Imprinting and ANPSI: An attempt to replicate Peoc'h. *Journal of the Society for Psychical Research* 55: 417–419.

Jung, C. G. (1971). *Psychological types.* Princeton: Princeton University Press.

Jürgenson, F. (1964). *Rosterna fran Rymden.* Stockholm: Saxon & Lindström Förlag.

_____. (1980). *Telefone para o além.* São Paulo: Civilização Brasileira.

K

Kagan, J. (2002). *Surprise, uncertainty and mental structures.* Cambridge, MA: Harvard University Press.

Kalitzin, S., and Suffczynski, P. (2003). Comments on "Correlations between brain electrical activities of two spatially separated human subjects," Wackermann et al. (2003). *Neuroscience Letters* 350: 193–194.

Kastenbaum, R. (1988). *Haverá vida depois da morte?* Lisbon: Caravela.

_____. (2011). *Death, society, and human experience.* 11th ed. New York: Routledge.

Keil, H., and Tucker, J. (2005). Children who claim to remember previous lives: Cases with written records made before the previous personality was identified. *Journal of Scientific Exploration* 19(1): 91–101.

Kellehear, A. (1993). Culture, biology, and the near-death experience: A reappraisal. *The Journal of Nervous and Mental Disease* 181(3): 148–156.

Kelly, E., Kelly, E., Crabtree, A., Gauld, A., Grosso, M., and Greyson, B. (2007). *Irreducible mind: Toward a psychology for the 21st century.* Lanham, MD: Rowman & Littlefield.

Kelly, E. W. (2010). Some directions for mediumship research. *Journal of Scientific Exploration* 24(2): 247–282.

Kelly, E. W., and Arcangel, D. (2011). An investigation of mediums who claim to give information about deceased persons. *Journal of Nervous and Mental Disease* 199(1): 11–17.

Kilner, W. J. (1993). *A aura humana.* São Paulo: Pensamento.

King, J. (2009). *World transformation: A guide to personal growth and consciousness.* Bloomington, IN: AuthorHouse.

Kirlian, S. D., and Kirlian, V. (1963). *Photography and visual observation by means of high-frequency currents.* Springfield, VA: National Technical Information Service.

Klemenc-Ketis, Z. (2013). Life changes in patients after out-of-hospital cardiac arrest. *International Journal of Behavioral Medicine* 20(1): 7–12. DOI: https://doi.org/10.1007/s12529-011-9209-y.

Klemenc-Ketis, Z., Kersnik, J., and Grmec, S. (2010). The effect of carbon dioxide on near-death experiences in out-of-hospital cardiac arrest survivors: A prospective observational study. *Critical Care* 14(2): 1–7. DOI: https://doi.org/10.1186/cc8952.

Korotkov, K., Matravers, P., Orlov, D., and Williams, B. (2010). Application of electrophoton capture (EPC) analysis based on gas discharge visualization (GDV) technique in medicine: A systematic review. *The Journal of Alternative and Complementary Medicine* 16(1): 13–25.

Krieger, D. (1975). Therapeutic touch: The imprimatur of nursing. *American Journal of Nursing* 75(5): 784–787.

Krishnamurti, J. (1999). *Meditações.* Lisbon: Presença.

Bibliography

L

Laberge, S., Levitan, L., Brylowsi, A., and Dement, W. (1988). "Out-of-body" experiences occurring in REM sleep. *Sleep Research* 17: 115.

Lancastre, M. J. (1981). *Fernando Pessoa—Uma Fotobiografia.* Lisbon: Imprensa Nacional-Casa da Moeda.

Laozi, and Chan, W.-T. (1963). *The way of Lao Tzu (Tao-te Ching).* Translated with introductory essays, comments, and notes by Wing-Tsit Chan. New York: Macmillan College Publishing Company.

Leadbeater, C. W. (1902). *Man, visible and invisible.* London: Theosophical.

Le Maléfan, P. (1992). Naissance du parapsychologique chez Max Dessoir, philosophe et médecin (1867–1947). *Frenesie* 10: 237–248.

Levin, J. (2011). Energy healers: Who they are and what they do. *Explore: The Journal of Science and Healing* 7(1): 13–26.

Lewis, H. S. (1930). *Mansions of the soul: The cosmic conception.* San Jose, CA: Rosicrucian, AMORC College.

Lobach, E., and Bierman, D. (2004). Who's calling at this hour? Local sidereal times and telephone telepathy. *Proceedings of Parapsychology Association Annual Convention* (Vienna), 91–97.

Locher, T. and Harsch, M. (1995). *Les contacts ver l'au-delà à l'aide de moyens techniques existent!* Poix de. Picardie, France: Parasciences.

Lucas, W. (1993). *Regression therapy: A handbook for professionals.* Crest Park, CA: Deep Forest.

M

MacRae, A. (2005). Report of an electronic voice phenomenon experiment inside a double-screened room. *Journal of the Society for Psychical Research* 69: 191–201.

Manolea, A. (2015). Brain to brain connectivity during distal psycho-informational influence sessions, between spatially and sensory isolated subjects. *Procedia-Social and Behavioral Sciences* 187: 250–255.

Marino, A., Becker, R., Ullrich, B., and Hurd, J. (1979). Kirlian photography: Potential for use in diagnosis. *Psychoenergetic Systems* 3: 47–54.

Maslow, A. (1970). *Motivation and personality.* 2nd ed. New York: Harper & Row.

Masters, K. S., Spielmans, G., and Goodson, J. (2006). Are there demonstrable effects of distant intercessory prayer? A meta-analytic review. *Annals of Behavioural Medicine* 32(1): 21–26.

Mattos, L. (1983). *Pela verdade: A acção do espírito sobre a matéria.* 9th ed. Rio de Janeiro: Centro Redentor.

May, E., Utts, J., Humphrey, B., Luke, W., Frivold, T., and Trask, V. (1990). Advances in remote-viewing analysis. *Journal of Parapsychology* 54: 193–228.

McClenon, J. (1982). A survey of elite scientists: Their attitudes toward ESP and parapsychology. *Journal of Parapsychology* 46(2): 127–152.

Miles, P., and True, G. (2010). Reiki—Review of biofield therapy history, theory, practice, and research. *Alternative Therapies* 9(2): 62–72.

Mills, A. (1990). Moslem cases of the reincarnation type in Northern India: A test of the hypothesis of imposed identification. Part I: Analysis of 26 cases. Part II: Reports of three cases. *Journal of Scientific Exploration* 4: 171–202.

_____. (2003). Are children with imaginary playmates and children said to remember

Bibliography

previous lives cross-culturally comparable categories? *Journal of Transcultural Psychiatry* 40: 62–90.

Mills, A., and Tucker, J. (2015). Reincarnation—Field studies and theoretical issues today. In *Parapsychology—A handbook for the 21st century*, ed. E. Cardeña, J. Palmer and D. Marcusson-Clavertz (Jefferson, NC: Mcfarland), 314–326.

Moody, R. (1975). *Life after life*. New York: Bantam.

Morales, P. R. (2004). *Evidências—Morte, reencarnação, carma*. Curitiba, Brazil: Rosacruz.

Moreira-Almeida, A. (2004). *Fenomenologia das experiências mediúnicas, perfil e psicopatologia de médiuns espíritas*. PhD thesis. Faculty of Medicine, Saint Paul University, Brazil. DOI: https://doi.org/10.11606/T.5.2005.tde-12042005-160501.

_____. (2012). Research on mediumship and the mind-brain relationship. In *Exploring the frontiers of the mind-brain relationship*, ed. A. Moreira-Almeida and F. S. Santos (New York: Springer), 191–213.

_____. (2013). Explorando a relação mente-cérebro: Reflexões e diretrizes. *Revista Psiquiatria Clínica* 40(3): 105–109.

Morse, M., Castillo, P., Venecia, D., Milstein, J., and Tyler, D. C. (1986). Childhood near-death experiences. *American Journal of Diseases of Children* 140(11): 1110–1114. DOI: https://doi.org/10.1001/archpedi.1986.02140250036031.

Morse, M., Conner, D., and Tyler, D. (1985). Near-death experiences in a pediatric population: A preliminary report. *American Journal of Diseases of Children* 139: 595–600.

Morse, M., and Perry, P. (1992). *Do outro lado da vida: O que nos ensinam as experiências de quase-morte de crianças*. Rio de Janeiro: Objetiva.

Moulton, S. T., and Kosslyn, S. M. (2008). Using neuroimaging to resolve the psi debate. *Journal of Cognitive Neuroscience* 20(1): 182–192.

Moura, G. (2000). *Protótipo de software para o diagnóstico de aspectos psicológicos baseados nas fotos Kirlian*. Bachelor thesis, Regional University of Blumenau—Center of Exact and Natural Sciences, Brazil. Available at: http://dsc.inf.furb.br/arquivos/tccs/monografias/2000-1gilbertocesarmouravf.pdf.

Murray, C. D., Howard, T., Wilde, D. J., Fox, J., and Simmonds-Moore, C. (2007). Testing for telepathy using an immersive virtual environment. *Journal of Parapsychology* 71: 105–123.

N

Nash, C. (1982). Psychokinetic control of bacterial growth. *Journal of the Society for Psychical Research* 51(790), 217–221.

Nelson, K., Mattingly, M., Lee, S. A, and Schmitt, F. A. (2006). Does the arousal system contribute to near death experience? *Neurology* 66(7): 1003–1009.

Neppe, V. M. (2002). Out of body experiences (OBEs) and brain localisation: A perspective. *Australian Journal of Parapsychology* 2(2): 85–96.

Newton, M. (1995). *La vida entre vidas*. Barcelona, Spain: Robinbook.

Nunes, C. S. (1990). *Transcomunicação—Comunicações tecnológicas com o mundo dos "mortos."* São Paulo: Edicel.

O

Osho, B. S. R. (2004). *Consciência—A chave para viver em equilíbrio.* Cascais, Portugal: Pergaminho.

Osis, K., and Haraldsson, E. (1997). *At the hour of death: A new look at evidence for life after death.* Norwalk, CT: Hastings.

Owens, J., Cook, E. W., and Stevenson, I. (1990). Features of "near-death experience" in relation to whether or not patients were near death. *Lancet* 336(8724): 1175–1177. DOI: https://doi.org/10.1016/0140-6736(90)92780-L.

P

Palmer, J. A. (2001). *Parapsychology and the Rhine Research Center.* Durham, NC: Parapsychology.

Parnia, S. (2006). *What happens when we die—A groundbreaking study into the nature of life and death.* Carlsbad, CA: Hay House.

Parnia, S., Waller, D. G., Yeates, R., and Fenwick, P. (2001). A qualitative and quantitative study of the incidence, features and aetiology of near death experiences in cardiac arrest survivors. *Resuscitation* 48(2): 149–156. DOI: https://doi.org/10.1016/S0300-9572(00)00328-2.

Pasricha, S. K., Keil, J., Tucker, J., and Stevenson, I. (2005). Some bodily malformations attributed to previous lives. *Journal of Scientific Exploration* 19: 359–383.

Peoc'h, R. (1988). Chicken imprinting and the tychoscope: An ANPSI experiment. *Journal of the Society for Psychical Research* 55: 1–9.

_____. (1995). Psychokinetic action of young chicks on the path of an illuminated source. *Journal of Scientific Exploration* 9: 233–229.

_____. (2001). Chick's distant psychokinesis (23 kilometres). *Revue Française de Parapsychologie* 11(1): 1–5.

Pérez-Navarro, J. M., and Guerra, X. M. (2012). An empirical evaluation of a set of recommendations for extrasensory perception experimental research. *Europe's Journal of Psychology* 8(1): 32–48.

Playfair, G. L. (1999). Identical twins and telepathy. *Journal of the Society for Psychical Research* 63: 86–98.

Portela, L. (1994). *Para além da evolução tecnológica.* Porto, Portugal: ASA.

_____. (1997). *À janela da vida.* Porto, Portugal: ASA.

_____. (1999). *Esvoaçando.* Porto, Portugal: ASA.

_____. (2004). *Encarar a realidade.* Porto, Portugal: ASA.

_____. (2014). *Serenamente.* 4th ed. revista e atualizada. Lisbon: Gradiva.

_____. (2015). *O prazer de ser.* 4th ed. Lisbon: Gradiva.

_____. (2019). *Ser espiritual—Da evidência à ciência.* 29th ed. Lisbon: Gradiva.

Pratt, J. G., and Keil, H. (1973). Firsthand observations of Nina S. Kulagina suggestive of PK upon static objects. *Journal of the American Society for Psychical Research* 67: 381–390.

Presi, P. (2006, September). *The work at Il Laboratorio.* Paper presented at the American Association—Electronic Voice Phenomena (AA-EVP) Conference, Atlanta, Georgia. http://atransc.org/presi-il-laboratorio/.

Bibliography

R

Radin, D. (1997). *The conscious universe: The scientific truth of psychic phenomena.* New York: HarperCollins.

_____. (2002). Exploring relationships between random physical events and mass human attention: Asking for whom the bell tolls. *Journal of Scientific Exploration* 16(4): 533–547.

_____. (2004). Event-related electroencephalographic correlations between isolated human subjects. *The Journal of Alternative and Complementary Medicine* 10(2): 315–323.

_____. (2006). *Entangled Minds—Extrasensory Experiences in a Quantum Reality.* New York: Pocket.

Radin, D. and Ferrari, D. (1991). Effects of consciousness on the fall of dice: A meta-analysis. *Journal of Scientific Exploration* 5(1): 61–83.

Radin, D., Schlitz, M., and Baur, C. (2015). Distant healing intention therapies: An overview of the scientific evidence. *Biofield Science and Healing: Toward a Transdisciplinary Approach* 4: 67–71.

Ramacharaca, Y. (1998). *A vida depois da morte.* São Paulo: Pensamento.

Ramos, A. C. (2016). *Contributo do Reiki no bem-estar do recém-nascido com cólicas abdominais.* Master's thesis, Évora University—São João de Deus School of Nursing, Portugal. http://hdl.handle.net/10174/19469.

Raudive, K. (1971). *Breakthrough: An amazing experiment in electronic communication with the dead.* Gerrards Cross, UK: Colin Smythe.

Reece, K., Schwartz, G. E., Brooks, A. J., and Nangle, G. (2005). Positive well-being changes associated with giving and receiving Johrei healing. *The Journal of Alternative and Complementary Medicine* 11(3): 455–457.

Rhine, J. B. (1971). Location of hidden objects by a man-dog team. *Journal of Parapsychology* 35: 18–33.

Rhine, J. B., and Brier, R. (1984). *Parapsicologia atual.* Saint Paul, Portugal: Cultrix.

Rhine, L. E., and Rhine, J. B. (1943). The psychokinetic effect: I. The first experiment. *Journal of Parapsychology* 7: 20–43.

Richards, T.L., Standish, L.J., Kozak, L., and Johnson, C. (2005). Replicable functional magnetic resonance imaging evidence of correlated brain signals between physically and sensory isolated subjects. *Journal of Alternative and Complementary Medicine* 11(6): 955–963.

Ring, K. (1980). *Life at death: A scientific investigation of the near-death experience.* New York: Coward, McCann and Geoghegan.

Ritchie, G. (1991). *My life after dying.* Norfolk, VA: Hampton Roads.

Ritchie, G., and Sherrill, E. (1987). *Voltar do amanhã.* Lisbon: Caravela.

Roberts, R., and Groome, D. (2001). *Parapsychology—The science of unusual experience.* New York: Oxford University Press.

Rocha, A., Paraná, D., Freire, E., Lotufo Neto, F., Moreira-Almeida, A. (2014). Investigating the fit and accuracy of alleged mediumistic writing: A case study of Chico Xavier's letters. *Explore: The Journal of Science and Healing* 10(5): 300–308.

Rock, A. J. (2014) (Ed.). *The survival hypothesis: Essays on mediumship.* Jefferson, NC: McFarland.

Roe, C., Sonnex, C., and Roxburgh, E. (2015). Two meta-analyses of noncontact healing studies. *Explore: The Journal of Science and Healing* 11(1): 11–23. DOI: https://doi.org/10.1016/j.explore.2014.

Bibliography

Roney-Dougal, S. and Solfvin, J. (2002). Field study of enhancement effect on lettuce seeds: Their germination rate, growth and health. *Journal of the Society for Psychical Research* 66: 129–143.

Rouder, J., Morey, R., and Province, J. (2013). A Bayes factor meta-analysis of recent extrasensory perception experiments: Comment on Storm, Tressoldi, and Di Risio (2010). *Psychological Bulletin* 139(1): 241–247.

S

Salazar, A. (1915). *A diferenciação sistemática do pallium cerebral.* Porto, Portugal: Tipografia da Enciclopédia Portuguesa.

Schäfer, H. (1992). *Théorie et pratique de la tanscommunication: Un pont entre notre monde et l´au-delà.* Paris: Éd. Robert Laffont, S.A.

Schmidt, S., Erath, D., Ivanova, V., and Walach, H. (2009). Do you know who is calling? Experiments on anomalous cognition in phone call receivers. *The Open Psychology Journal* 2: 12–18.

Schmidt, S. Schneider, R., Utts, J., and Walach, H. (2004). Distant intentionality and the feeling of being stared at: Two meta-analyses. *British Journal of Psychology* 95(2): 235–247.

Schouten, S., and Stevenson, I. (1998). Does the socio-psychological hypothesis explain cases of the reincarnation type? *The Journal of Nervous and Mental Diseases* 186(8): 504–506.

Schwaninger, J., Eisenberg, P. R., Schechtman, K. B., and Weiss, A. N. (2002). A prospective analysis of near-death experiences in cardiac arrest patients. *Journal of Near-Death Studies* 20(4): 215–232. DOI: https://doi.org/10.1023/A:1015258818660.

Schwartz, G. (2002). *The after life experiments: Breakthrough scientific evidence of life after death.* New York: Pocket Books.

_____. (2012). Consciousness, spirituality, and postmaterialist science: An empirical and experiential approach. In *The Oxford Handbook of Psychology and Spirituality*, ed. L. Miller (New York: Oxford University Press), 584–596.

Schwarz, J. H. (1998). Recent developments in superstring theory. *Proceedings of the National Academy of Sciences of the United States of America* 95(6): 2750–2757. DOI: https://doi.org/10.1073/pnas.95.6.2750.

_____. (2010). Status of superstring and m-theory. *International Journal of Modern Physics A: Particles and Fields; Gravitation; Cosmology; Nuclear Physics* 25(25), 4703–4725.

Schwarz, P. M., and Schwarz, J. H. (2004). *Special relativity—From Einstein to strings.* Cambridge, UK: Cambridge University Press.

Segalowitz, S. J. (2007). Knowing before we know: Conscious versus preconscious top-down processing and a neuroscience of intuition. *Brain and Cognition* 65: 143–144.

Senkowski, E. (1995). *Instrumentelle transkcommunikation (Instrumental transcomunication).* Frankfurt, Germany: R. G. Fischer Verlag.

Sheldrake, R. (1998). Perceptive pets with puzzling powers: Three surveys. *International Society for Antrozoology* 15: 2–8.

_____. (2004). *The sense of being stared at.* London: Hutchinson.

_____. (2009). *A new science of life.* London: Icon.

_____. (2011). *Dogs that know when their owners are coming home, and other unexplained powers of animals.* 2nd ed. New York: Three Rivers.

Bibliography

_____. (2014). Telepathy in connection with telephone calls, text messages and emails. *Journal of International Society of Life Information Science* (ISLIS) 32(1): 7–10.

Sheldrake, R., and Smart, P. (1998). A dog that seems to know when his owner is returning: Preliminary investigations. *Journal of the Society for Psychical Research* 62(850), 220–232.

_____. (2000a). A dog that seems to know when his owner is coming home: Videotaped experiments and observations. *Journal of Scientific Exploration* 14(2): 233–255.

_____. (2000b). Testing a return-anticipating dog, Kane. *Anthrozoös* 13(4): 203–212.

Shroder, T. (1999). *Old souls—The scientific evidence for past lives.* New York: Simon & Schuster.

Silva, A. (1988). *Considerações e Outros Textos.* Lisbon: Assírio & Alvim.

Simões, M. (2003). Parapsicologia—Uma perspectiva crítica. In *Psicologia da consciência: Pesquisa e reflexão em psicologia transpessoal,* ed. M. Simões, M. Resende and S, Gonçalves (Lisbon: Lidel), 233–245.

Snow, C., and Wambach, H. (1989). *Mass dreams of the future.* New York: Mcgraw-Hill.

Solovitch, S. and Henricot, M. (1992). Remembrance of traumas past. *Omni* 15(2): 46–51.

Spanos, N. P., Menary, E., Gabora, N. J., DuBreuil, S. C., and Dewhirst, B. (1991). Secondary identity enactments during hypnotic past-life regression: A socio-cognitive perspective. *Journal of Personality and Social Psychology* 61: 308–320.

Standish, L., Johnson, L., Kozac, L., and Richards, T. (2003). Evidence of correlated functional magnetic resonance imaging signals between distant human brains. *Alternative Therapies in Health and Medicine* 9(1): 128, 122,125.

Standish, L., Kozak, L., Johnson, L. C., and Richards, T. (2004). Electroencephalographic evidence of correlated event-related signals between the brains of spatially and sensory isolated human subjects. *The Journal of Alternative and Complementary Medicine* 10(2): 307–314.

Stevenson, I. (1970). A communicator unknown to medium and sitters. *Journal of the American Society for Psychical Research* 64: 53–65.

_____. (1973). A communicator of the "drop in" type in France: The case of Robert Marie. *Journal of the American Society for Psychical Research* 67: 47–76.

_____. (1974). *Twenty cases suggestive of reincarnation.* 2nd ed. Charlottesville, VA: University of Virginia Press.

_____. (1976). A preliminary report of a new case of responsive xenoglossy: The case of Gretchen. *Journal of the American Society for Psychical Research* 70: 65–77.

_____. (1977). The explanatory value of the idea of reincarnation. *Journal of Nervous and Mental Disease* 164: 305–326.

_____. (1980). *Cases of the reincarnation type: Twelve cases in Lebanon and Turkey* (Vol. 3). Charlottesville, VA: University Press of Virginia.

_____. (1983). *Cases of the reincarnation type: Twelve cases in Thailand and Burma* (Vol. 4). Charlottesville, VA: University Press of Virginia.

_____. (1987). *Children who remember previous lives: A question of reincarnation.* Charlottesville, VA; University Press of Virginia.

_____. (1993). Birthmarks and birth defects corresponding to wounds on deceased persons. *Journal of Scientific Exploration* 7(4): 403–410.

_____. (1994). A case of the psychotherapist's fallacy: Hypnotic regression to "previous lives." *American Journal of Clinical Hypnosis* 36(3): 188–193.

_____. (1997a). *Biology and reincarnation: A contribution to the etiology of birthmarks and birth defects.* Westport, CT: Praeger.

_____. (1997b). *Where reincarnation and biology interse*ct. Westport, CT: Praeger.

_____. (2003). *European cases of the reincarnation type.* Jefferson, NC: McFarland.

Stickgold, R., Hobson, J. A., Fosse, R., and Fosse, M. (2001). Sleep, learning and dreams: Off-line memory reprocessing. *Science* 294(5544): 1052–1057.

Storm, L. (2003). Remote viewing by committee: RV using a multiple agent/multiple percipient design. *Journal of Parapsychology* 67: 325–342.

Storm, L., Tressoldi, P., and Di Risio, L. (2010). Meta-analysis of free-response studies, 1992–2008: Assessing the noise reduction model in parapsychology. *Psychological Bulletin* 136(4): 471–485.

Storm, L., Tressoldi, P., and Utts, J. (2013). Testing the Storm et al. (2010) meta-analysis using Bayesian and frequentist approaches: Reply to Rouder et al. (2013). *Psychological Bulletin* 139(1): 248–254.

Strübin, B. (1996). *Reiki—Force universelle de vie.* Romont, Switzerland: Editions Recto-Verseau.

T

Tarazi, L. (1997). *Under the inquisition: An experience relived.* Charlottesville, VA: Hampton Roads.

Tart, C. (1963). Possible physiological correlates of psi cognition. *International Journal of Parapsycholoy* 5: 375–386.

_____. (2009). *The end of materialism: How evidence of the paranormal is bringing science and spirit together.* Oakland, CA: New Harbinger.

_____. (2011). Out-of-the-body experiences. In *Psychic exploration: A challenge for science, understanding the nature and power of consciousness*, ed. E. D. Mitchel, J. White, M. Schlitz and D. Radin (New York: Cosimo), 349–374.

Trismegistus, Hermes (2013). *The Emerald Tablet of Hermes.* US: Merchant Books.

Tucker, J. (2007). *A vida antes da vida.* Lisbon: Sinais de Fogo.

_____. (2008). Children's reports of past-life memories: A review. *Explore: The Journal of Science and Healing* 4(4): 244–248.

_____. (2016). The case of James Leninger: An American case of the reincarnation type. *Explore: The Journal of Science and Healing* 12(3): 200–207.

Tucker, J., and Nidiffer, F. (2014). Psychological evaluation of American children who report memories of previous lives. *Journal of Scientific Exploration* 28: 583–594.

U

Ulbricht, C., Basch, E., Bent, S., Chao, W., Costa, D., Che, W-D., ... Weissner, W. (2010). Evidence-based review of Qi Gong by the natural standard research collaboration. *Natural Medicine Journal* 2(5): 7–15.

Ullman, M., and Krippner, S. (1989). *Dream telepathy: Experiments in nocturnal ESP.* 2nd ed. Jefferson, NC: McFarland.

Underhill, E. (1955). *Mysticism: A study in the nature and development of man's spiritual consciousness.* New York: Noonday.

Bibliography

V

Van Lommel, P. (2006). Near-death experience, consciousness and the brain: A new concept about the continuity of our consciousness based on recent scientific research on near-death experience in survivors of cardiac arrest. *World Futures* 62: 134–152. DOI: https://doi.org/10.1080/02604020500412808.

_____. (2011). *Consciousness beyond life—The science of the near-death experience.* New York: HarperOne.

Van Lommel, P., Van Wees, R., Meyers, V., and Elfferich, I. (2001). Near-death experience in survivors of cardiac arrest: A prospective study in the Netherlands. *Lancet* 358(9298): 2039.

W

Wackermann, J., Seiter, C., Keibel, H., and Walach, H. (2003). Correlations between brain electrical activities of two spatially separated human subjects. *Neuroscience Letters* 336(1): 60–64.

Walach, H., Bosch, H., Lewith, G., Naumann, J., Schwarzer, B., Falk, S., ... Bucher, H. (2008). Effectiveness of distant healing for patients with chronic fatigue syndrome: A randomised controlled partially blinded trial (EUHEALS). *Psychotherapy and Psychosomatics* 77(3): 158–166.

Walsh, N. (2003). *Conversas com Deus—3.* Cascais, Portugal: Sinais de Fogo Publicações.

Wambach, H. (1978). *Reliving past lives: The evidence under hypnosis.* New York: Harper & Row.

Wang, F., Man, J., Lee, E., Wu, T., Benson, H., Fricchione, G., ... Yeung, A. (2013). The effects of Qigong on anxiety, depression and psychological well-being: A systematic review and meta-analysis. *Evidence-Based Complementary and Alternative Medicine.* Article ID 152738. DOI: https://doi.org/10.1155/2013/152738.

Watt, C. (2016). *Parapsychology: A beginner's guide.* London: Oneworld.

Weil, P. (2005). *Rumo ao infinito.* Petropolis, Brazil: Vozes.

Weisensale, B. (1981). Shielding a recorder from radio frequency interference for EVP. *Spirit Voices* 3. Republished: American Association of Electronic Voice Phenomena web site.

Weiss, B. (1988). *Many lives, many masters: The true story of a prominent psychiatrist, his young patient, and the past-life therapy that changed both their lives.* New York: Fireside.

_____. (1993). *Through time into healing: Discovering the power of regression therapy to erase trauma and transform mind, body and relationships.* New York: Fireside.

_____. (1997). *Only love is real: A story of soulmates reunited.* New York: Grand Central.

_____. (2004). *Same soul, many bodies: Discover the healing power of future lives through progression therapy.* New York: Free Press.

Wilber, K. (1993). *Psicología Integral.* Barcelona: Kairós.

Woolger, R. J. (1988). *Other lives, other selves: A Jungian psychotherapist discovers past lives.* New York: Doubleday.

Z

Zukav, G. (2014). *The seat of the soul.* New York: Simon & Schuster.

Index

Index

Index

Index